ALL FIFTY-TWO CARDS

By Marshall Miles

How to Win at Duplicate Bridge
All Fifty-two Cards

ALL FIFTY-TWO CARDS

*How to Reconstruct
the Concealed Hands
at the Bridge Table*

BY

MARSHALL MILES

FOREWORD BY RICHARD L. FREY

An Exposition–Banner Book

EXPOSITION PRESS   NEW YORK

First Printing, May, 1963
Second Printing, June, 1963
Third Printing, September, 1963
Fourth Printing, November, 1963

EXPOSITION PRESS INC., 386 Park Avenue South, New York 16

FIRST EDITION

EP 41117

Foreword

AWAY FROM the bridge table, Marshall Miles is an unassuming young man. In fact, you might even call him modest, if there were such a thing as a modest bridge expert. But when he plays bridge or writes about it, he assumes his full stature as a player who knows every trick in the game and who knows, also, how to coach his readers in the art of winning those tricks.

Generally, it is safe to assume that only an instruction book for beginners or players of limited experience will have a wide sale. This one, however, is likely to be the exception. True, to get the most out of it requires some previous knowledge and experience in the game; the more your experience, the more you are apt to appreciate the finer points Miles makes as he trots out example after example of situations where a little thought can be worth hundreds upon hundreds of extra points.

But this is the kind of book that will interest any fan who likes to read about fascinating hands and who doesn't mind occasionally finding that there was more to the situation than he himself was able to see until Miles pointed it out.

As the pages fly by, however, the reader will find himself "seeing" the right thing to do more and more often—not because the hands become easier but because he is learning the way of thinking that all experts follow. If you are a perceptive reader, suddenly a whole new world will open up, expanding the 36-by-36 square of the bridge table to a boundless arena of intellectual pleasure and greater skill.

When that happens, you will wish this generous book had twice as many pages as it actually has.

RICHARD L. FREY

Acknowledgments

I WISH to thank many friends for their help in the production of this book. First—at least in order of time—is my regular and favorite partner, Eddie Kantar. I am indebted to him for many of the hands used here. Some of them he played. On other occasions he spotted interesting plays and problems that others overlooked —often of the sort that did not occur but would have occurred with a different opening lead or other bidding.

The second person who has rendered invaluable assistance is Barbara Tepper, who volunteered to edit the book. She made many beneficial changes in construction, organization, and style. That sort of editing required bridge ability, writing ability, and lots of hard work.

I am also indebted to someone whom I have never met. I wanted a fairy tale as an introduction, and, at Barbara Tepper's request, Barbara Alpren produced one for me.

M. M.

Contents

An Introductory Fable

By Barbara P. Alpren

Once upon a time there were two brothers who lived in downtown Asia Minor. They were just a couple of ordinary guys who played very average bridge. Even their names were not unusual—Harry and Billie Sol Aladdin.

Every night for a thousand and one nights they played bridge at the club, but their game never seemed to improve. After twenty-eight years they were becoming a trifle discouraged. Luckily their wives were very discerning; a dozen of them chipped in and bought the boys a copy of *Technique for a Sheik*, the hottest bridge book in the Middle East.

"Oh, goody, just what I've always wanted!" cried Harry in true Turkish delight. "Here's a chapter called 'Tenace, anyone?'—a romance about a poor man capturing a queen."

"I can't wait to start memorizing these percentage tables," said Billie Sol. "This technical jazz could be the open sesame to our success. We'll be rich quicker than you can say Scheherazade!"

For weeks the Aladdins practiced improving their technique. They squeezed and finessed as the good book said. Finally they were ready to make a killing in the two-cent game at the club.

Alas! Every rubber was a financial fiasco. Queens eluded them on two-way finesses and adverse trumps defied probability by splitting four to one. Penniless and crushed, they slunk out into the Arabian night.

"A lot of good technique did us!" muttered Billie Sol on the way home.

"Forget it, kid," said Harry. "Let's sing. Maybe it will make us feel better."

They had barely started "I Dream of Genie With the Light Brown Hair" when, out of a puff of smoke, Mr. Clean materialized!

"You called, non-masters?" asked the genie. "What can I do for you, sires?"

"Teach us how to win at bridge!" they cried.

"Elementary, *effendi*," he replied. "I'll teach you how to reconstruct the concealed hands. Soon you'll be able to figure out what everyone has."

"It sounds too easy to be true," said Harry.

"It *is*," said the genie with a modest blush. "That's why my clients call my system 'How to Succeed in Bridge Without Really Spying.'"

The new system worked like a charm. One year later the Aladdins had become so famous and rich that the Summer Nationals were held in Billie Sol's living room!

(N.B. Any similarity between the moral of this fable and the following book is purely intentional.—B. P. A.)

Introduction

IN ORDER TO play or defend well at bridge, it is necessary to visualize all fifty-two cards, not just the twenty-six cards you can see in your own hand and dummy. This visualization can be accomplished in a number of ways: by "counting," analyzing the bidding, interpreting the information partner is sending, and drawing inferences from the way the opponents are playing or defending. Frequently it is necessary to "place" certain cards arbitrarily and to play on the assumption that the cards are distributed in this manner. The justification for doing so is that your play will gain if your assumption is correct, and it will not lose if it is incorrect. For example, with ace-queen opposite two small, you normally finesse the queen even when you have no clue regarding the location of the king. You take the finesse because it will gain a trick if the king is on side, and you will still take the one trick to which you are entitled if the queen loses to the king.

This is not an orthodox bridge book. Nowhere will you find a percentage table or a chart of standard opening leads. This book will not tell you how to play A Q 9 x opposite x x x x, nor does it advocate any bidding methods, either old or new. It is, instead, a guide toward playing and defending hands to better advantage, using only the material you have in your present repertoire. The methods described in this book are not new. They do not require any prodigious feats of memory or talent. They represent the processes which lead the expert toward making "lucky guesses" and "killing defenses." It will teach the average player to get more out of his cards merely by coordinating and applying the information already available to him at the table.

A few of the hands in this book were made up to illustrate a point. Most of the hands were actually dealt and played, although minor changes have sometimes been made to clarify the point being discussed and to avoid side issues. Usually the bidding is given just as it took place. Since this is not a book on bidding, I have seldom commented upon it unless it had some bearing upon the play. The fact that no comment has been made does not necessarily imply that I approve of the bidding. When bad bidding has created an interesting problem in the play or defense, so much the better!

This book is divided into five chapters covering the five main methods of reconstructing the unseen hands. The last four chapters all give methods of determining the actual holdings. The first chapter does not seem to fit into the pattern. Instead of enabling you to determine the actual hands, it advises you to make certain assumptions and to place the cards arbitrarily where you want them to be (or don't want them to be!). There are two justifications for this technique. It enables you to eliminate mental effort by rejecting from consideration holdings where your play is immaterial, and it enables you to make the right play. For example:

NORTH
- ♠ 8 6
- ♡ Q J 8 7 3
- ◇ A 5 4
- ♣ 7 5 4

Bidding

EAST	SOUTH	WEST	NORTH
Pass	1 ♡	Pass	2 ♡
Pass	4 ♡	Pass	Pass
Pass			

SOUTH
- ♠ A Q
- ♡ A K 9 6 2
- ◇ K Q 6
- ♣ 9 8 2

West leads the king of clubs, followed by the queen. East overtakes the queen with the ace and cashes the jack, West discarding a high spade. East then shifts to a low spade. Will the finesse work? I don't know, but it is not worth stewing over. You have no reason to believe that the finesse will work, but you also have nothing to lose by taking it.

The play of the hands is described in the present tense and is presented to you in the form of a problem. Don't just take the easy way of reading along to see what comes next. Act as if you were playing or defending, and see what you can figure out as the play is described. Try to keep ahead of the text and reconstruct the unseen hands before you are told how to do it. Whether your solution is correct or not, you will benefit from the instruction and remember the solution best if you have made a genuine effort to solve the problem on your own.

M. M.

ALL FIFTY-TWO CARDS

CHAPTER I

Playing on an Assumption

IT IS necessary to make many assumptions in the play and defense. For example:

A player who has bid spades has at least four.
When dealer passes, he does not have fourteen points.
A defender who leads a queen has at least the jack of
that suit, but not the king.

While assumptions of this type are occasionally false, they are usually true and reliable because there is a logical reason for them. They are *not* the type of assumption which is the subject of the present chapter.

If this were a book on logic or mathematics, I would carefully define terms and avoid giving more than one meaning to the word "assumption." The type just discussed would be referred to as "an inference" or as "an assumption supported by evidence," while the new type of assumption would be called "an arbitrary assumption." But this is a book on bridge, and I am not a crusader, so I shall use the same word in two different ways, just as other bridge players do.

In the Introduction I explained that whenever you take a finesse, you assume that it will work (whether or not you *believe* it will work). I also implied that you should assume that it will work, because you would gain by taking it if it should work and would lose nothing by taking it if it should not work. As a practical matter, that is not quite true.

Sometimes you assume that the cards lie a certain way because there is *very little* to lose if they do not. Suppose that you are in a six-heart contract with the following hands:

NORTH
♠ A Q 5
♡ A K 8 4
◊ 7 5
♣ K 8 4 3

SOUTH
♠ 6
♡ J 10 7 5 3 2
◊ A 8
♣ A Q J 6

You win the opening diamond lead with the ace and play a trump. West shows out—which means that you will have to lose a trump trick. Obviously your proper play is to cash two high trumps, return to your hand with a club, and take the spade finesse in order to discard the losing eight of diamonds. You assume that the spade finesse will work because you need it to make your contract. It is true that a losing finesse would cause you to be set two tricks, thereby losing an additional 50 or 100 points, but that is an insignificant amount compared to the bonus for making game and slam.

The general rules for playing on an assumption are as follows:

1. If the cards must lie a certain way for you to make your contract, assume that they lie that way.
2. If the cards must lie a certain way for your contract to be in danger, assume that they lie that way (and take appropriate precautions).
3. Make no more assumptions than are necessary; it is easier to have one prayer answered than two.
4. Consider all of the consequences of your assumption; if the consequences are ridiculous or improbable, try making a different assumption.
5. When defending on an assumption, follow the same principles, with defeat of the contract as your objective. (Assume a lie of the cards which will enable you to defeat the contract.)

If all these rules are not perfectly clear to you, don't worry. They will be after you have studied the following examples. Ready?

Declarer Play

NORTH
♠ A Q J 7 3
♡ 8 7 4
◇ 5
♣ K Q 8 7

SOUTH
♠ 4
♡ A 9 5 2
◇ K 7
♣ A J 10 6 5 4

The opening lead is a heart against your optimistic six-club contract. How good are your chances? Not very good, are they? Three losing hearts have to be disposed of. The only chance to obtain three discards is to find West with K x x of spades so that a finesse plus one ruff will yield four spade tricks. Consequently, you should assume that the spades lie just that way.

If the finesse loses, you will be set three tricks instead of one or two, but that shouldn't deter you. Six clubs down one or two tricks would not be a satisfactory result at either rubber bridge or duplicate.

NORTH
♠ 8 7 6 5
♡ K
◇ K J 8 6 5 4 2
♣ 5

SOUTH
♠ A K 4
♡ A Q J
◇ 7 3
♣ A 10 9 6 4

Again you are in an optimistic contract—three no-trump—and to make matters worse, West kills the only sure entry to dummy by leading a heart. You overtake the king and lead a low diamond. West plays the ten. What should you play from dummy?

At duplicate, this would be a real problem (because your objective is to beat other pairs—not necessarily to make your contract), but at rubber bridge you have no choice. You must duck completely! The only chance to make three no-trump is to run the diamond suit, and the only chance to run the diamond suit is for East to have the singleton ace. With the doubleton ace, for example, he would refuse to take the first trick if you were to finesse the jack. It would be correct to duck even if West had played the queen at the first trick (a very cute play with Q 10 9!). The only reason for overtaking the first heart and leading a diamond toward the dummy was to give the opponents an opportunity to make a mistake. So far as your legitimate chances were concerned, you could have led a low diamond away from dummy at trick two just as effectively.

NORTH
♠ K 8 4
♡ Q 9 5 3
◇ K 7 3
♣ 8 6 5

SOUTH
♠ A
♡ K 8 7 2
◇ A Q 6 4
♣ Q J 4 2

West leads the jack of spades against your four-heart contract. Since there are two sure club losers, you must find a way to avoid the loss of two trump tricks. The best chance is to play one of the defenders for a doubleton ace of hearts by leading low to an honor and ducking on the way back. Because of the shortage of entries to dummy (and with no clue as to the location of the ace), the best play is to lead a low heart from your own hand immediately. West plays the jack, and the queen loses to East's ace.

The holding you were playing for (doubleton ace with West) does not exist on this hand, but the fact that West played an honor gives you another chance. East returns a spade, which you win in dummy, discarding a club.

At this point, you have a choice of plays to pick up the trump suit without further loss. You can go up with the king, hoping that West started with the doubleton jack-ten, or you can finesse through East on the assumption that the jack of hearts was a singleton. If the contract were no-trump, the finesse would be the percentage play (you will just have to take my word for this statement), but at hearts, you have no real choice.

The correct play is to go up with the king, because if the heart finesse should work, the contract would be unmakeable! Suppose that East started with A 10 x x of hearts. If four rounds of trumps were played, the defenders would be able to cash a spade trick upon gaining the lead with a high club. Nor would it do any good to leave the trumps out. South could not ruff a spade and also pick up East's ten of hearts.

The correct play succeeds. West had the jack-ten of hearts doubleton. Incidentally, can you spot an error in the defense? East should have played small without hesitation, allowing the queen of hearts to win! Then declarer would have ducked a heart on the way back, playing West for the doubleton ace-jack instead of the doubleton jack-ten.

In none of the preceding hands was there any indication that the cards lay just right. You had to assume the most favorable distribution, since if your assumption turned out wrong, you could not make the contract anyway. In the next example you have to make a different sort of assumption.

```
     NORTH
  ♠ 8
  ♡ K J 5                          Bidding
  ◇ 10 9 8 6 3         SOUTH   WEST   NORTH   EAST
  ♣ A K 8 4           1 ♡    Pass    2 ◇     2 ♠
                      Pass    3 ♠     4 ♡     4 ♠
     SOUTH            Pass    Pass    5 ♣     Pass
  ♠ 6 3              5 ♡    Pass    Pass    Pass
  ♡ A 9 7 4 3 2
  ◇ A K
  ♣ Q 7 2
```

West leads a small spade. East wins with the ace and returns the nine of clubs. This time the contract looks easy—almost too easy. What can happen to defeat five hearts? East may have all four trumps. That is very unlikely, since he must have great length in spades, and if he does have four trumps, nothing can be done about it. Forget that possibility. There is no purpose in worrying about defeat when it is unavoidable.

What is the next-worse distribution? *West* may have all four trumps. Can anything be done about that? Yes, a first-round finesse of the jack of hearts can be taken. It would be wrong to cash the ace first, because the opponents could later force you to ruff a spade with the jack of hearts. If the heart finesse should lose, you wouldn't care (at rubber bridge, anyway), for you would still make your contract. So you should play on the assumption that West has all four trumps. His actual hand:

♠ K 10 x   ♡ Q 10 8 6   ◇ Q x   ♣ J 10 8 x

NORTH				
♠ K 9 5				
♡ 8 6	*Match-point duplicate: bidding*			
◇ K J 10 7	**SOUTH**	**WEST**	**NORTH**	**EAST**
♣ 9 8 4 2	2 ♡	2 ♠	2 NT	4 ♠
	5 ♡	5 ♠	Pass	Pass
SOUTH	6 ♡	Pass	Pass	Pass
♠ —				
♡ A K Q 10 7 5 2				
◇ A Q 8 4 3				
♣ 6				

The opening lead is the queen of spades, covered by the king and ace. You ruff and lay down the ace of hearts. West discards a spade. What should you play next? It looks as though this is a pianola—just lead a diamond to dummy, take the marked heart finesse, and cash your tricks. Is there any distribution where this play could be wrong? Only if East should be void of diamonds, in which case he would ruff, lead a club to his partner, and get another ruff.

It takes a real pessimist to worry about the possibility that East is void of diamonds, but it cannot cost anything to lead a club first to take care of that possibility. This cuts the communication between the defenders and limits East to one trump trick. You should assume the worst, since it makes no difference what you do if the worst does not occur. Actually "the worst" is not too bad since the opponents are cold for six spades, and down one your way should be a very good result. The East-West hands are

EAST: ♠ A x x x   ♡ J x x x   ◇ —   ♣ K J 10 x x
WEST: ♠ Q J 10 x x x   ♡ —   ◇ x x x x   ♣ A Q x

NORTH
♠ A Q 8 5
♡ Q 10 8 6
◇ 7 5   *Bidding*
♣ A Q 6   WEST   NORTH   EAST   SOUTH
                           1 ◇   Double   Pass   2 ♠
SOUTH   Pass   4 ♠   Pass   Pass
♠ J 7 4 3 2   Pass
♡ A J 3
◇ A 6 3
♣ 8 4

This is rubber bridge, and West leads the king of diamonds. Let us anticipate the material contained in the next chapter and see whether we can figure out what West has for his opening bid. His diamond bid and lead mark him with king-queen of diamonds plus either the jack or ten. If he has a five-card suit, as indicated by East's play of the deuce, he could have a skimpy opening bid with just two kings on the side. East should have either one king or no kings. With this much help, do you see how to play the hand? If not, give East each of the various kings and see what will happen. If his king is the king of spades, the heart finesse will fail and the club finesse will work. Result: making four spades by losing a spade, a heart, and a diamond.

Before figuring further, win the opening lead and take the spade finesse, knowing that if it does *not* work, you are sure to make your contract.* The spade finesse works, but East shows out on the second round. Now suppose that East has the king of hearts. You would then make five, losing just a spade and a diamond. If East's king is the king of clubs, you could lose a trick in each suit. If you were sure that East had the king of clubs, you would hop right up with the ace of clubs when West

---

* If East should win the spade finesse and return a diamond, he might conceivably overruff dummy on the third round. However, this is a remote possibility because (*a*) most likely East has no king; (*b*) he probably does not have a doubleton diamond, especially since he played the deuce.

returns a club after winning the heart finesse. That way, you would still make your contract provided West could not ruff in before you should discard your club loser on the fourth heart. But it is quite likely that East has no king, and you would feel foolish to refuse the club finesse, let West ruff the third round of hearts and cash the king of clubs.

What can you do to increase your chances? The key play is to lead a heart to the ace and a low heart—not the jack—toward dummy. If East wins, you will have given up a trick by refusing the heart finesse, but then the club finesse must work. You will only have given away an overtrick. If West wins immediately and returns a club, take the finesse, playing East for no kings. But you have an added chance this way. If West has K x x of hearts, he may duck the second round of hearts! He would figure that you were missing the jack (otherwise, why didn't you finesse?), and he might play low quickly, hoping that you would play the ten from dummy. If you can steal a heart trick, you will know what to do. By continuing the third round of hearts, you will have an absolute cinch for the contract.

In the following hand, a new type of assumption is involved. At rubber bridge your only concern is to make the maximum profit or suffer the minimum loss on each hand. When the contract is not doubled, making the contract when a declarer or defeating the contract when defending is your primary objective. In a doubled contract, you are only concerned with how much a particular play can gain or lose and how likely it is to work.

In duplicate bridge, however, your objective is to beat other pairs. If you think you are in an exceptionally good contract, you play safe, just as in rubber bridge. You have already beaten most of the other pairs with your bidding, and you don't want to risk losing your advantage by a dangerous line of play. If you are in a bad contract or an unusual contract, you must assume that the cards lie in such a manner as to permit you to get a good result.

NORTH
♠ J 7 6 4
♡ J
♢ K 8 7 5 3
♣ 8 6 2

Match-point duplicate,
neither side vulnerable: bidding

EAST	SOUTH	WEST	NORTH
1 ♡	1 ♠	4 ♡	4 ♠
Double	Pass	Pass	Pass

SOUTH
♠ A K 9 5 2
♡ A 10 8
♢ 9 4
♣ 7 5 4

West leads the four of hearts. East plays the queen, and you win with the ace. How do you like your contract? Not very well, do you?

The opponents have an excellent chance to set you three tricks. On the other hand, if you are "lucky" enough for the spades to split 2–2, or if the king of diamonds is on side, then you surely could have set four hearts. In that event, even a 300-point set would be a bad result. Nor can you expect many teams to be in the same boat, since partner's four-spade bid was quite optimistic. Is there any distribution of the opponents' cards which could make four spades a good sacrifice? If there is, you must play for it. Your best chance is that West has a single-ton spade. The correct play is to ruff a heart and return the jack of spades, intending to let it ride if not covered. The four hands might be

NORTH
♠ J 7 6 4
♡ J
♢ K 8 7 5 3
♣ 8 6 2

WEST
♠ x
♡ 9 x x x x
♢ Q x
♣ A Q J 10 x

EAST
♠ Q 10 x
♡ K Q x x
♢ A J 10 x
♣ K x

SOUTH
♠ A K 9 5 2
♡ A 10 8
♢ 9 4
♣ 7 5 4

Obviously, if East covers the jack of spades, you will return to dummy for another trump finesse. The double spade finesse is not a bad play even at rubber bridge when you consider the bidding, but at duplicate it is mandatory.

NORTH
♠ A Q 8
♡ K J 8 4
◊ A 6
♣ K 10 9 5

SOUTH
♠ 7 6
♡ A Q 10 7 3
◊ 7 4 2
♣ A J 6

While it is necessary to make certain assumptions, it is unwise to make more assumptions than necessary. West leads a low spade against your six-heart contract. You finesse the queen, which holds. After drawing trumps, you assume that West has the queen of clubs and take the club finesse through him. It works, and you make six hearts.

Are you proud of yourself? You should bury your head in shame! It was necessary to guess who had the queen· of clubs, but the spade finesse was a horrible play. It gained nothing when it worked and could have been very costly if it had lost. Your losing spade would go on the fourth round of clubs. If you had decided to play East for the queen of clubs, you would have taken a first round finesse in order to get four club tricks and a discard of the losing spade.

NORTH
♠ A 6 5
♡ A 7 3
◇ A K J 9
♣ A Q 4

SOUTH
♠ 3
♡ K 9 6 2
◇ 8 6 3
♣ K J 10 8 6

Bidding

EAST	SOUTH	WEST	NORTH
Pass	Pass	1 ♠	Double
Pass	3 ♡	Pass	3 ♠
Pass	4 ♣	Pass	6 ♡
Pass	Pass	Pass	

West leads the king of spades. The first assumption you must make is that the trumps split favorably. Otherwise there will be no play for this contract. Assuming a 3–3 trump split, you can count one spade trick, three heart tricks, two diamond tricks, and five club tricks, for a total of eleven. Will the diamond finesse be necessary also? Not if you make the most of your first assumption—that trumps split 3–3. Win the ace of spades and ruff a spade, followed by a low trump lead, ducked in dummy. If the opponents return a trump, win with the king. Enter dummy with a minor suit winner and ruff dummy's last spade. Then enter dummy with a winner in the other minor suit to pull the outstanding trumps with the ace, and discard dummy's diamonds on the clubs.

If the opponents return anything but a trump at trick four, the order of cashing tricks is changed slightly, but you still play for a dummy reversal! A dummy reversal looks far-fetched with A 7 3 of trumps in the dummy, but it is entirely logical when you realize that you need a 3–3 split anyway. There is no necessity for making the additional assumption that the diamond finesse will work.

NORTH
♠ A Q J 10 3
♡ 8 7 4
◇ 5
♣ K Q 8 7

SOUTH
♠ 4
♡ A 9 5 2
◇ K 7
♣ A J 10 6 5 4

The opening lead is a heart against your optimistic six-club contract. Does this hand look familiar? It is the same as the first hand of the chapter with only one card changed—dummy has the ten of spades instead of the seven. This one "minor" change makes all the difference in the world.

Now it is no longer correct to lead a low spade toward dummy and finesse. In order for this play to work, not only must West have the king but it must be only twice guarded (K x x). By playing the ace and taking a ruffing finesse through East, you can make your contract whether East has K x x x, K x x, or the king alone.

The point is that either East or West may have the king. In order to make your contract, you must guess who has it, and a guess is a form of assumption. However, if you decide to play West for the king, you must make an additional assumption: that he has no more than three spades. The more assumptions you make, the more likely that one of them will be wrong. If this is not clear to you, consider this example from the field of sports. The football teams from Army and Notre Dame are scheduled to play each other next Saturday, and according to the odds-makers, it should be an even match. Suppose that someone were to offer you this peculiar betting proposition: "I'll bet you even money and let you pick the team, but if you pick Army, you will also have to decide how many points Army will win by." If you were inclined to bet, you would undoubtedly pick Notre Dame.

One of the shortcomings of the average player is that he does not fully consider the consequences of his assumptions and reject them when they lead to absurd results.

NORTH
♠ K 8 6 4
♡ K 10 9 5
♢ J 9 4 3   *Bidding*
♣ A

SOUTH	WEST	NORTH	EAST
1 ♡	Pass	3 ♡	Pass
4 ♡	Pass	Pass	Pass

SOUTH
♠ 9 5 2
♡ A Q 8 6 3 2
♢ A Q
♣ Q 6

West leads the four of clubs. Upon winning with the ace, you draw trumps with the ace and king, West discarding the deuce of clubs on the second round. Now you take the diamond finesse, which loses. West returns the queen of spades, which you duck, and East plays the seven. West continues with the jack of spades. What do you play from dummy? And why? When this hand was actually played, declarer ducked again, explaining afterwards that he was playing East for the doubleton ace. Ducking was wrong for several reasons. In the first place, if West held Q J 10 x of spades to start with, he surely would have preferred to lead a spade on opening lead from a sequence rather than a club from a longer, broken suit, whether it was headed by the king or the jack. The most obvious reason why it was correct to cover was that it could not gain to duck even if the ace were doubleton. East would be unable to continue the suit, and the losing spade could be discarded on the jack of diamonds. Unfortunately, South gave the wrong reason for his bad play. He should have said that he was playing West for the doubleton queen-jack! West's actual hand:

♠ A Q J   ♡ 7   ♢ K 8 5 2   ♣ J 9 7 4 2

NORTH
♠ K 10 8 4
♡ K 7 3
♢ 8 7 3
♣ A 7 5

Bidding

WEST	NORTH	EAST	SOUTH
1 ♢	Pass	Pass	2 ♠
Pass	4 ♠	Pass	Pass
Pass			

SOUTH
♠ A Q J 7 3 2
♡ A J 9
♢ 10 6 2
♣ J

West leads the king of diamonds and continues with the queen and a small diamond. East wins the third round with the ace and returns the ten of clubs, covered by the jack, queen, and ace. You draw the opponents' trumps, West discarding the jack of diamonds on the second round. Now what?

There are three possibilities for avoiding a heart loser. The first assumption which naturally comes to mind is that East has the queen, in which case a simple finesse would work. Let us test that assumption. West's hand would be something like

♠ x   ♡ 10 x x   ♢ K Q J x   ♣ K Q x x x

which is a very dubious opening bid, and East would have failed to keep the bidding open with

♠ x x   ♡ Q x x x   ♢ A x x   ♣ 10 9 8 x.

Rather than assume that both opponents have bid abnormally, you should try a different assumption. Suppose that West has the doubleton queen or queen-ten of hearts. This would leave East with

♠ x x   ♡ x x x x x   ♢ A x x   ♣ 10 9 x.

Some players might have bid one heart with this hand; others might not. Let us see what West would have. You know that he had four diamonds and one spade. If he had a doubleton heart, his whole hand would be

♠ x   ♡ Q x   ♢ K Q J x   ♣ K Q x x x x.

Surely he would have bid one club rather than one diamond
with that hand. So this assumption also must be rejected. When
you test the third assumption—that West has the queen of hearts,
and East has the ten—you find nothing wrong with it, so it is
the one you must adopt. You lead the jack of hearts and, if
covered, finesse the nine on the way back.

Defense

NORTH
♠ A 4
♡ A 5
◇ A 6 4
♣ Q 10 9 7 6 3

EAST
♠ 8 6 5
♡ J 9 7 6 2
◇ 9 8 5
♣ K 2

Rubber bridge: bidding

NORTH	EAST	SOUTH	WEST
1 ♣	Pass	2 NT	Pass
3 NT			

Partner leads the queen of spades, winning the trick. He
continues with a small spade, won by dummy's ace. A low club
is led from dummy. If you are alert, you hop up with the king
and return a spade. The only chance to set this contract, consistent with the bidding, is to find partner with the ace of clubs.
If so, you must win the first club trick and return a spade while
partner still has an entry. You must assume that declarer's hand
is something like this:

♠ K x x   ♡ K Q x   ◇ K J x x   ♣ J x x

```
                NORTH
                ♠ K 8
                ♡ 9 8 6
                ◇ K Q J 7 4          EAST
                ♣ K Q 2              ♠ 9 7
                                     ♡ A Q J 7 5 3
                                     ◇ 8 6
                                     ♣ A J 3
```

Bidding

NORTH	EAST	SOUTH	WEST
1 ◇	2 ♡	2 ♠	3 ♡
3 ♠	Pass	4 ♠	

Partner leads the deuce of hearts, and your ace drops declarer's ten. You wish partner had led the king of hearts on which you would have played low. Partner would shift to a club, and you would duck when dummy played the queen. Then if partner could regain the lead, another club return would defeat the contract.

Enough wishful thinking! Partner did not lead the king of hearts, so you must return a low club, playing him for the ten—as well as the ace of diamonds or a trump trick.

```
                        NORTH
                        ♠ Q 9                Bidding
                        ♡ 9 4              SOUTH    NORTH
        WEST            ◇ A Q J 8 4         1 ♣      1 ◇
        ♠ K J 7 2       ♣ Q J 6 5          1 ♠      3 ♣
        ♡ J 10 7 6 3                        3 NT
        ◇ 7 5
        ♣ K 4
```

Your opening lead is a low heart, partner's king falling to declarer's ace. Declarer leads a low diamond to the jack, which holds. He then leads the queen of clubs, which you win with the king. At this point declarer is marked with ace-queen of hearts, king of diamonds, and ace of clubs—consequently ten

tricks unless you can take the setting tricks in spades. (Partner
could not logically be holding off with the king of diamonds because there are plenty of entries to dummy, and his proper play
would be to win immediately and return a heart before your
entries were eliminated.)

In order to set the contract you must assume, at least, that
partner has the ace of spades. If partner has the ace of spades,
will you be able to take four spade tricks? Not necessarily. If
declarer has four spades headed by the ten, or even the eight,
he will have a fourth round stopper unless you are careful, and
if he has both the ten and eight, the situation is hopeless. Correct play is to cash the king, upon which partner will unblock
his middle card with A 10 x or A 8 x. Then a low card is led
to the ace, and a spade return will go through declarer's tenace.

You have already been advised not to make more assumptions than necessary. That is another way of saying not to make
any assumption that is unnecessary. Suppose that a contract
can be defeated if partner has either of two cards. You should
try not to base your entire defense on the possibility of his holding one specific card.

```
                    NORTH
                 ♠ K J 8 5
                 ♡ 8 6
                 ◇ 5 3                      EAST
                 ♣ K Q 9 7 6             ♠ 10 4
                                         ♡ J 9 7 3
                                         ◇ A 6 2
                                         ♣ 8 5 4 2
```

Rubber bridge: bidding

NORTH	EAST	SOUTH	WEST
Pass	Pass	1 ♠	Pass
3 ♠	Pass	4 ♠	Pass
Pass	Pass		

Partner leads a trump. Declarer wins, cashes another round
of trumps, and leads the jack of clubs. Partner takes the ace

and returns a diamond to your ace. Declarer obviously has plenty of tricks in the black suits unless the defenders can cash two more tricks in the red suits. If partner has the king of diamonds, he still needs the ace of hearts as a setting trick, and if he does not have the king of diamonds, he needs the ace-queen of hearts—plus a heart return by you. You assume that partner has one of those holdings, so you return a heart to take care of both possibilities.

<pre>
                          NORTH
                          ♠ 9 6
                          ♡ A Q 10 7 4
            WEST   ◇ K J 10
         ♠ A J 8 3   ♣ A Q 6
         ♡ K 8 5
         ◇ Q 5
         ♣ 10 8 7 3
</pre>

Bidding

NORTH	EAST	SOUTH	WEST
1 ♡	Pass	1 NT	Pass
2 NT	Pass	3 NT	Pass
Pass	Pass		

Your opening lead is a small spade, partner's ten forcing the king (but you know declarer also has the queen). Next, declarer leads the jack of hearts. Unless the jack is singleton (in which case the contract will almost certainly be defeated whatever you do), declarer has five heart tricks, a spade trick, and the ace of clubs. If he also has the king of clubs or ace of diamonds, he will have nine tricks.

So the first assumption to make is that partner has both the king of clubs and ace of diamonds. If partner has these two cards, will the contract be defeated automatically? Think this over carefully. Suppose that you duck the jack of hearts. If declarer continues hearts, he can run the suit, but when he gets through, he will have to lead away from dummy, and he will be helpless. If he shifts to a diamond after the jack of hearts holds, he can establish two or more diamond tricks by finessing the ten, but he will be unable to re-enter his hand to use them or to take another heart finesse. However, if you cover the heart, and if declarer has the nine, he can return to his hand for the diamond finesse. His hand might be

♠ K Q 9   ♡ J 9 x   ◇ 9 8 x x   ♣ J x x.

You must play partner for the ace of diamonds, the king of clubs, and more than one heart, but it is unnecessary to play him for the nine of hearts. Consequently you should duck the jack.

NORTH
♠ 10
♡ J 8 6 3
◇ A J 9
♣ J 9 7 3 2

WEST
♠ K 9
♡ K 10 7 2
◇ K 10 4
♣ A 10 8 6

Bidding

NORTH	EAST	SOUTH	WEST
Pass	Pass	2 ♣	Pass
2 ◇	Pass	2 ♠	Pass
3 NT	Pass	4 ♠	Pass

The opening two-club bid and two-diamond response were artificial, the strong part of the "weak two bid" system. This is not an easy hand to lead from. You choose the deuce of hearts, and partner's nine forces the ace. Declarer plays the ace and queen of spades, partner following to both rounds and dummy discarding a club.

What do you know about declarer's hand? Before reading further, how many spades do you think he has? The fact that he is missing so many high cards is an indication that he has **tremendous spade length** to compensate, but the surest clue

was his play of the spade suit. With only seven spades to the
ace-queen-jack (missing the nine), it would be a foolish play
for him to lay down the ace. Even if he should catch the singleton king, he would still have to lose a trick to the nine-spot, and
if there were a singleton other than the king, it would cost him
a trick to waste the ten. So declarer, if he is a reasonable player,
is marked with an eight-card spade suit. Seven of those eight
spades are winners, and you can see two red aces for nine tricks.

It is hard to imagine even a ladies' afternoon two-bid without
the king of clubs, so you must assume that declarer does not have
the queen of clubs or queen of diamonds (unless it is a singleton). Once you have come to this conclusion, it is logical to
exit with a low heart to take care of the possibility that declarer
started with eight spades, two hearts, a singleton diamond
(which might be the queen) and king-small of clubs. If declarer
ruffs this trick, and leads a low diamond, whether immediately
or later, you must insert the king to kill the dummy.

Declarer actually held

♠ A Q J x x x x x ♡ A ◇ x x ♣ K x.

As you can see, it would be fatal to play low on the first round
of diamonds.

		NORTH	
		♠ 5	
		♡ K Q 7 2	
	WEST	◇ A Q 8 6 3	
	♠ K Q 8	♣ 9 6 4	
	♡ 10 9 8 6 3		
	◇ J 5 2		
	♣ A 3		

Bidding

EAST	SOUTH	WEST	NORTH
1 ◇	1 ♠	2 ♡	Pass
2 NT	Pass	3 NT	Double
Pass	4 ♣	Double	Pass
Pass	Pass		

Your opening lead is a small diamond. Dummy's ace wins
and declarer discards a spade. A low heart is led from dummy,
won by declarer's jack, and a heart is returned and ducked, won
by partner's ace. A low trump is returned, declarer putting up
the queen. Now what? Declarer is marked with eleven black
cards, presumably six spades and five clubs. If you return a
trump, partner can win the first spade trick with his marked ace
and return another trump.

Can anything possibly go wrong? Suppose declarer had five
spades and six clubs. Then he would win the club return and
give up a spade. He would ruff a spade and discard his remaining two spades on dummy's high hearts—making four clubs
doubled! Rather than risk a catastrophe you should assume the
worst and let partner ruff a heart winner. You can win the first
spade trick and return a trump. Caution pays off because declarer's hand was

♠ 10 9 x x x   ♡ J x   ◇ —   ♣ K Q 10 x x x.

It might be noted that declarer's play in discarding a spade and
playing hearts rather than trying for immediate spade ruffs was
a clue to his actual distribution.

		NORTH
		♠ A K Q
		♡ 6 4
WEST		◇ A Q 10 5 3 2
♠ 9 6		♣ K 3
♡ K Q 10 8 7 5 2		
◇ 8		
♣ Q 10 5		

Rubber bridge,
both sides vulnerable: bidding

EAST	SOUTH	WEST	NORTH
Pass	Pass	2 ♡	Double
Pass	3 NT	Pass	Pass
Pass			

On your opening lead of the king of hearts, partner discards the jack of spades, and declarer wins with the ace. He leads a low diamond, finessing the queen, and partner's king wins. Partner returns a spade. The ace of diamonds is then cashed, declarer discarding a heart.

What can you tell about the distribution of declarer's hand? You know for sure that he started with four hearts since partner had none, and you know that he started with just one diamond because he showed out on the second round. How many spades should declarer have? Either two or three, not more. If partner had only four spades, he would not have discarded the jack on the first trick. Declarer's most probable distribution is three spades, four hearts, one diamond and five clubs.

The king of clubs is played from dummy with partner and declarer playing small. You must play a club honor, hoping that partner started with J 9 x. If you play a small club, declarer can cash another of dummy's spades and toss you on lead with either the second or third round of clubs. You would then have to lead a club or a heart, permitting him to use his long clubs.

If declarer cashes a spade and leads a club to his ace, you must, of course, unblock the queen. It is your only hope to set the hand, and it actually works since declarer's club holding was A 8 x x x.

The following hand is from the 1962 Spingold knock-out team of four. See if you can do better than the actual West player did.

                                        NORTH
                                        ♠ 9 2
                                        ♡ A Q 10 9
        WEST   ◇ 9 7 3
    ♠ Q 8 6 5 4 3   ♣ K 9 5 4
    ♡ K 6
    ◇ 10 6 4 2
    ♣ 3

                            Bidding
        SOUTH   WEST   NORTH   EAST
         2 ♣*   Pass   2 ♡   Pass
         3 ◇   Pass   4 ◇   Pass
         5 ♣   Pass   5 ♡   Pass
         6 ◇   Pass   Pass   Pass

        * Strong but artificial

You lead the deuce of trumps, won by dummy's seven, as
partner discards a heart. The nine of hearts is led from dummy,
partner playing small, and declarer discarding a spade! Can
you figure out the other hands, and can you see the best defense?

Let's start with diamonds. You know that declarer's holding
was A K Q J x x, which means that he has six cold diamond
tricks. Since the nine of hearts is driving out your king, you can
see two heart tricks. Surely declarer has the two black aces for
the bidding (also for his play; can you imagine his ducking the
nine of hearts if he is missing a black ace?), and consequently
eleven tricks. Only partner can have a stopper in hearts and
clubs. Consequently he will be squeezed unless you can find a
way to break up the squeeze. If declarer has A J x x of clubs,
his contract is cinched. Your only hope is to lead a club to
break up the squeeze, hoping that partner has the queen and
jack of clubs. Sure enough, he does, and a club return defeats
the contract. Declarer's hand:

        ♠ A J x   ♡ —   ◇ A K Q J x x   ♣ A 10 x x

CHAPTER II

Deductions From Bidding

YOUR ANALYSIS of the opponents' bidding (or failure to bid) must be influenced by your opinion of their skill and style. In other words, you cannot expect them always to bid the same as you do. Many players use this as an excuse not to analyze the bidding at all. Have you ever had the following experience?

After partner has unsuccessfully defended a hand, you point out that his line of defense could not work unless declarer had held five spades and four hearts to the ace-queen, despite the fact that he bid nothing but spades on three rounds of bidding. Partner then pulls you aside and explains that Mr. Jones is such an unreliable bidder that he could easily have had 5-4-3-1 distribution instead of his actual 6-3-3-1. This argument about Mr. Jones' unreliability never impresses me. The truth is that partner was not thinking or counting, and he has shown more imagination in the post-mortem than he did on defense.

My experience has convinced me that the opponents' bidding is much more reliable than their play. Every bridge player can count up to thirteen (points, not tricks!), and everyone likes to bid. The poor player may not always make the same bid as you, but he usually makes *some* bid with a biddable hand—and he is likely to bid his longest suit. An important consideration is that if you make a play based upon a logical analysis of the bidding, and this play goes wrong, you can join in the laughter whenever the hand is discussed later.

But suppose you base your play upon an assumption that an opponent has done something peculiar or stupid. When it turns out that the opponent was bidding or playing quite properly, you will never enjoy discussing the hand as much as do your partner and friends. On this cynical note, let's look at some hands.

NORTH
♠ 7 3
♡ A J 4 2
◇ K Q J 6 5
♣ K J

SOUTH
♠ A K 5
♡ Q 7 3
◇ 10 9 7 2
♣ Q 10 6

Suppose that you are the declarer, playing a three no-trump contract, with no adverse bidding. The opening lead is the jack of spades. You duck, and West continues with the eight of spades, upon which East plays the queen. You win and lead a diamond to knock out the ace. West wins and leads another spade. Dummy discards a heart. East plays a spade, and you win. At this point you can count only seven tricks—four diamonds, two spades, and a heart.

You have two possibilities for the two additional tricks. The obvious and correct play is to lead a club to establish two club tricks. Though you have no more stoppers in spades, you will make your contract if the spades split 4–4 or if the defender with the long spades does not have the ace of clubs. The other possibility is to finesse the jack of hearts. However, since you need two additional tricks, a winning heart finesse will not do you any good unless the king drops under the ace next time. If the finesse loses, you can be set even though the spades are split 4–4.

Now suppose the bidding has been as follows:

Bidding

WEST	NORTH	EAST	SOUTH
1 ♠	Double	Pass	2 NT
Pass	3 NT	Pass	Pass
Pass			

The play to the first four tricks has gone the same. Now the second alternative, which was decidedly inferior with no bidding, is the only correct line of play. The spades should be split 5–3 because most players refuse to open a four-card major headed by the jack. Furthermore, West must have the ace of clubs for his opening bid. Since leading a club will result in almost certain defeat, the heart finesse is the only chance. Fortunately the bidding indicates that it will work. At first, though, it appears that the success of taking a heart finesse depends on finding West with a doubleton heart. However, if West has five spades, the king of hearts, and the minor-suit aces, he will be squeezed! The jack of hearts cannot retain his spades, the ace of clubs, and a guard to his king of hearts. West's hand:

♠ J 10 9 8 x   ♡ K x   ◊ A x   ♣ A x x x

NORTH
♠ Q J 8 2
♡ Q 10 3
◊ A 7 4
♣ K Q 8

Match-point duplicate: bidding

EAST	SOUTH	WEST	NORTH
1 ♡	1 ♠	Pass	2 NT
Pass	3 ♠	Pass	4 ♠

SOUTH
♠ A 10 7 6 4 3
♡ K
◊ K 8 5 2
♣ 9 4

A low heart is led, and the ten is played in order to induce East to play the jack. Your scheme does not work (perhaps because East does not have the jack) and East wins with the ace. He shifts to a low spade, and you take the finesse, for it looks as though he has the king for his opening bid. Besides, you don't want to let East talk you out of making the percentage play. The finesse works, and you pick up East's doubleton king.

At this point you have ten tricks. Now, what about an over-trick? You can be almost positive that East holds the ace of clubs. Not only does he need it for his opening bid (there are only 12 scattered points outstanding without it), but West might well have raised to two hearts with three or four hearts, a singleton spade, and the ace of clubs. So, as the ace of clubs is almost surely on your right, the only way to make two club tricks is to play West for the jack and ten. The correct play is to finesse the eight of clubs! If it drives out the ace, you have the rest of the tricks. Even if East wins with the ten or jack, you will not have lost anything. You will just have traded a club loser for a diamond loser. East's hand:

♠ K x   ♡ A x x x x   ◇ Q J 8   ♣ A x x

NORTH
♠ A 8 6
♡ 6 3
◇ 10 5 3
♣ A Q 7 4 2

SOUTH
♠ K Q J 7 3
♡ A 2
◇ A 8 7 6
♣ 9 3

Bidding

EAST	SOUTH	WEST	NORTH
1 ♡	1 ♠	Pass	2 ♠
Pass	3 ♠	Pass	4 ♠
Pass	Pass	Pass	

West leads the four of hearts, and East plays the queen. If the opponents could see all the hands, they would make dia-bolical false-cards, and you would never know what is going on. However, they have to give each other a considerable amount of information in order to defend well and you can rely on it most of the time. Here, for example, East might have K Q J 10 9 8 7 of hearts, and West might be leading the four from the five-four doubleton. But I would play the hand on the assump-tion that West has three or four hearts to the jack (since East's play of the queen denies the jack), and East has five or six to the king-queen. If East also has the king-queen-jack of diamonds, he could have a skimpy opening bid without the king of clubs, but the odds are, in my estimation, at least ten to one that he has it. The club finesse should not be taken when it has so little chance of working.

The proper play is to win the opening lead and to duck a club completely. After the opponents cash their heart winner and return a diamond, you lead a club to the ace, dropping the doubleton king, and ruff a low club. Then three rounds of trumps, ending in dummy, allow you to take two diamond discards on the queen and the long club. East held

♠ x x   ♡ K Q 10 x x   ◇ K Q x x   ♣ K x.

Proper analysis enabled you to make the hand by avoiding a finesse that was doomed to almost certain failure.

NORTH			
♠ A Q 9 7 2			
♡ A K Q		*Bidding*	
◇ 5	WEST	NORTH	EAST	SOUTH
♣ A 9 6 3	1 ◇	Double	1 ♡	Pass
	1 NT	Double	2 ◇	3 ♣
SOUTH	Pass	3 ◇	Pass	3 NT
♠ 6	Pass	5 ♣	Pass	Pass
♡ 8 7 2	Pass			
◇ Q 9 8 3				
♣ J 10 8 7 2				

West leads the nine of hearts. What can he have for his opening bid?

It is unlikely that West has both the ace and king of diamonds since he did not lead the king of diamonds. If he has the king-jack of spades and the ace-jack of diamonds, he still ought to have the king-queen of clubs for the opening bid and no-trump rebid (and we are not even sure that he has the jack of spades and jack of diamonds). West surely has a doubleton, at most, in hearts, so you cannot play three rounds of hearts without pulling the trumps, and you cannot afford to pull trumps with so much work to do. It looks as though the diamonds are

4–4 because of East's two-diamond bid, and West's most likely distribution is 4-2-4-3. You can almost reconstruct West's hand from the bidding and the opening lead. It is

♠ K J x x   ♡ 9 x   ◇ A J x x   ♣ K Q x.

With a knowledge of where the cards are, it is easy to see what the best chance is. The ace of spades should be cashed and the second round ruffed. Then a low club (not the jack) is led in the hope that West will not split his honors. Once the nine holds, you continue your business of establishing the fifth spade and ruffing diamonds, leaving the king-queen of trumps outstanding.

NORTH
♠ K J 8 4
♡ A
◇ J 7 6 5
♣ A 8 4 2

SOUTH
♠ 6 5 2
♡ Q 10 9 7 5 3 2
◇ 10
♣ K 10

Bidding

EAST	SOUTH	WEST	NORTH
Pass	Pass	Pass	1 ◇
Pass	2 ♡	Pass	Pass
Pass			

The two-heart bid is the weak jump response. The opening lead is a small club, won by dummy's ace. You cash the ace of hearts and lead a club to the king. At this point you have to guess how to play the trump suit. The right play would be to lead the ten if the king were doubleton or to lead the queen if the jack were doubleton. It is too early in the hand to tell who has what, so you mentally toss a coin and lead the queen. As it happens, it makes no difference since West discards a diamond and East wins. He returns a low diamond. West wins with the ace and returns the eight, East covering dummy's jack with the queen.

You ruff and lead the ten of hearts. East takes his jack and returns the king of diamonds. When you ruff this and pull his

last trump, you only have one trump left, so it would be disastrous to misguess the spades. When you lead a spade, West
plays low. Do you play the king or the jack? The clue is what
did not happen in the bidding. East failed to open the bidding
with K J x x of hearts and K Q 9 x of diamonds (and probably
a club honor since West would be unlikely to underlead the
queen-jack). Surely with the ace of spades he would have
opened. Consequently you must play the king of spades. East
actually held

♠ Q x ♡ K J x x ◇ K Q 9 x ♣ J x x.

NORTH

♠ A 6 3 2
♡ 7 4
◇ A Q J 5 4 2
♣ 7

Match-point duplicate,
East-West vulnerable: bidding

SOUTH

♠ 9 8 6 2
♡ 9 6
◇ 10 7 5 3
♣ A K Q

WEST	NORTH	EAST	SOUTH
Pass	1 ◇	Pass	1 ♠
2 ♡	2 ♠	Pass	Pass
Pass			

In my opinion it is usually unsound to bid a "worthless"
four-card suit, but in this case it seemed to be the least of evils.
West leads the king and ace of hearts, dropping the ten and
queen from his partner. Then he shifts to a club. Indications
are that West has a seven-card heart suit. It looks as though he
could not have the king of diamonds without opening the bidding. When you play the ace and a low trump East wins the
king, dropping his partner's doubleton queen, and he cashes the
jack. Now you are positive that the king of diamonds is off-side.
Not many players would pass with a seven-card heart suit to
the ace-king with a king on the side, but no one would pass
with a king and queen on the side. You win the club return
and play the third round upon which West shows out. Now you
know that he started with 2-7-2-2 distribution, and the king of

diamonds is singleton in the East hand. To have a little fun, you ruff your queen of clubs, as though by mistake. Then you are "stuck" in the dummy and have to play the ace of diamonds. Needless to say, there is some muttering by the opponents at their fate in playing against a hack who ruffs his own winner, gets stuck in the dummy and is forced to lay down the ace of diamonds rather than take a losing finesse.

NORTH
♠ 10
♡ J 6 4 2
◇ A K 9 2   *Both sides vulnerable: bidding*
♣ K 7 5 3

SOUTH	WEST	NORTH	EAST
1 ♡	4 ♠	5 ♡	Pass
Pass	Pass		

SOUTH
♠ 9 5
♡ A K 8 7 3
◇ Q 5
♣ Q J 9 6

West leads the king of spades and shifts to a diamond. How should you play the trump suit? Without any bidding, you would surely lay down the ace and king, hoping for a 2-2 break or a singleton queen. After the vulnerable four spade bid, showing at least a seven or eight card suit, a 2-2 heart break is not very likely. In fact, West is almost as likely to have a void in hearts as to have the doubleton queen. Suppose West has an eight-card suit. He could not have a doubleton in each of the remaining suits. If he has a singleton it is much more likely to be in hearts (where the opponents have a combined total of only four) than in diamonds (where they have a combined total of seven). To put it another way, West would have five cards other than spades while East would have eleven cards other than spades. East has more "room" in his hand for hearts (or diamonds or clubs) than West has. The correct play in hearts is to lead the jack from dummy. This will enable you to pick up the suit without loss whenever West has the singleton ten or nine. It will also enable you to save a trick when West has a void. It loses when

West's singleton is the queen or in the unlikely event that West has a doubleton queen or 10-9, or in the extremely unlikely event that East has a singleton queen or a void. Incidentally, how do you play A J x x opposite K 10 9 x x? With no clues whatever, the percentage play is to play the ace and king, hoping for a 2–2 split or a singleton queen. The percentage in favor of playing for a drop rather than a finesse is very slight, so with the flimsiest clue, you can afford to disregard the "percentage" play. If the bidding indicates that one player has a long suit, it usually pays to cash a high card and attempt a finesse through his partner. For example, if you know that West has five or six hearts to East's two or three hearts, and if you have to pick up the queen of spades with a combined holding of nine, you should play West for a singleton spade rather than expect a 2–2 split.

NORTH
♠ 6 5 2
♡ Q 9 8 5
◊ K J 3 2
♣ J 2

Rubber bridge, both sides vulnerable, North-South 30 part-score: bidding

SOUTH	WEST	NORTH	EAST
1 ♡	Pass	2 ♡	Pass
3 ♡	Pass	Pass	Pass

SOUTH
♠ Q J 9
♡ A K J 7 3 2
◊ 7 4
♣ A Q

West leads the king, ace, and a third spade, giving East a ruff. East returns a club. The queen holds, and you pick up the outstanding trumps. Now, how do you play the diamonds? You should play West for the queen rather than the ace. The clue again was *what did not happen* in the bidding. With five spades to the A K 10 and the ace of diamonds, West surely would have overcalled, especially since you had a part-score.

NORTH
♠ A 9 6 2
♡ K
◇ A 10 7 3   *Rubber bridge: bidding*
♣ Q 8 4 2

SOUTH	WEST	NORTH	EAST
1 ♠	Pass	3 ♠	Pass
4 NT	Pass	5 ♡	Pass
6 ♠	Pass	Pass	Pass

SOUTH
♠ K Q J 7 5
♡ 6
◇ K Q 8 5 2
♣ A J

West leads the ace of hearts and shifts to a trump. There
is no way to avoid the club finesse so you take it and it works.
Now, how do you handle the diamond suit? Obviously it makes
no difference unless all the outstanding diamonds are in one
hand, but if such is the case, you can pick up the suit by playing the first high diamond from the right hand. If either defender
were void in diamonds, who would it be? If it were East, he
should have doubled the final contract for an unusual lead. So
you play a diamond to the ace and, as it happens, West shows
out.

NORTH
♠ A K 9 2
♡ J 3   *Bidding*
◇ 10 9 5 4
♣ K 7 3

SOUTH	WEST	NORTH	EAST
1 ◇	1 ♡	1 ♠	Pass
2 ◇	Pass	3 ◇	Pass
3 NT	Pass	Pass	Double
Pass	Pass	Pass	

SOUTH
♠ 8 5
♡ K 6 4
◇ K Q J 8 7 6 2
♣ A

West leads the seven of hearts. Without the double, you
would put up the jack, hoping that West has led the seven

from a five- or six-card suit headed by the ace-queen, and hoping that he also has the ace of diamonds. The one thing you can be sure of is that East has a diamond stopper (which has to be the ace) for his double, so there is no point in playing the jack of hearts. You play small from the dummy and East plays the nine. How do you like that? Prospects do not look bright. If West has led from the ace-queen, this contract cannot be made. The only hope is that East has the queen-nine doubleton. However this is not an unreasonable hope. Such a heart holding combined with the ace of diamonds is just the sort of hand that would justify a double. Since you have left the jack in the dummy, you can afford to duck. East continues with the queen, and you duck again! Whatever the opponents do, they can only take their ace of diamonds, holding you to one overtrick. If East had played the queen to the first trick, it would have been much more obvious that you should duck. It is always disconcerting to the opponents at this point for you and your partner to start an argument over who should have redoubled.

NORTH
♠ 3
♡ K Q 6 5
◇ A K 9 8 5 2
♣ 7 4

SOUTH
♠ J 7 2
♡ A 10 9 3
◇ Q J 6 3
♣ A 6

Bidding

NORTH	EAST	SOUTH	WEST
1 ◇	1 ♠	2 ♡	2 ♠
4 ♡	4 ♠	Pass	Pass
5 ♡	5 ♠	Pass	Pass
6 ♡	Pass	Pass	Pass

After this rather heated bidding sequence, West leads a low spade. East wins with the ace and returns a low club which you win with the ace. East has done a lot of bidding without many high cards. He must have very unbalanced distribution including eleven or twelve black cards. There is no hope for this contract unless East has at least one heart. If he had a void in diamonds and one or more hearts, he would have doubled six hearts for a diamond lead. While normally you would expect hearts to split 3–2, such a split is very unlikely on this bidding. The proper play upon winning the ace of clubs is to lead the nine or ten of hearts for a first-round finesse! You cannot cash the ace first because you have to ruff a spade in dummy. Even if East has a doubleton heart, the odds are better than 50-50 that the finesse will work, as will be explained in the next chapter. The first round finesse is necessary to make the hand, for East's hand is

♠ A Q x x x   ♡ x   ◊ x   ♣ Q J x x x x.

Defense

```
          NORTH
      ♠ 6 2
      ♡ Q 8 5 4
      ◊ Q 10 9
      ♣ A J 10 3
                              EAST
                          ♠ 10 7 4 3
                          ♡ 9 6 2
                          ◊ A 7 5 3
                          ♣ Q 4
```

Bidding

SOUTH	WEST	NORTH	EAST
1 ♠	Pass	1 NT	Pass
2 ♡	Pass	3 ♡	Pass
4 ♡	Pass	Pass	Pass

Partner leads the deuce of diamonds, and you win dummy's nine with the ace. The lead of the deuce marks declarer with one more diamond, and he can get a discard by leading up to the queen in dummy. Declarer's bidding marks him with at least nine cards in the majors; with 4-4-3-2 distribution he would pass 1 no-trump or bid 3 no-trump over 3 hearts. A spade discard will not help him since he can ruff spades in the dummy, but if declarer has a small doubleton in clubs, it is important to shift to a club right away. Declarer actually has

♠ A K Q x x ♡ A J 10 x ◇ x x ♣ x x.

```
                              NORTH
                              ♠ 9 3
                              ♡ K Q 6 2
            WEST              ◇ K 7 4
            ♠ 10 7 5          ♣ 9 6 4 3
            ♡ 9 7
            ◇ Q J 10 2
            ♣ A Q 8 7
```

Match-point duplicate: bidding

SOUTH	WEST	NORTH	EAST
1 ♠	Pass	1 NT	Pass
2 ♡	Pass	3 ♡	Pass
3 ♠	Pass	4 ♡	Pass

You open the queen of diamonds, covered by the king and ace. Partner returns the three of diamonds, which means that he started with either two diamonds or four. Since South has almost surely indicated six spades and four hearts, he cannot have four diamonds. Besides, with four diamonds, declarer probably would not have played the king from dummy. So the bidding and partner's return indicate that declarer has no more diamonds and at most one club. Since he has only one club, it cannot lose anything for you to cash the ace, and it may be costly (at duplicate) not to, for you can see the spades lie favorably for the declarer. If he has six to the ace-king-jack or ace-queen-jack, he can discard dummy's entire club suit on the spades. Declarer's hand:

♠ A K J x x x ♡ A J x x ◇ x x ♣ x

If declarer has simply bid four hearts over three, you would wait with your club holding and play declarer for something like

♠ A K x x x ♡ A J x x ◇ x x ♣ K x.

In the following hand, the theme is slightly different. The defender should draw the correct inference from his *partner's* bidding in a competitive situation.

NORTH
♠ J 10 8 3
♡ K 6 2
◇ 7 5 2
♣ A Q 10

WEST
♠ A 9 7
♡ A 10
◇ J 10 9 8 6 4 3
♣ 9

Bidding

EAST	SOUTH	WEST	NORTH
1 ♠	4 ♡	4 ♠	5 ♡
Double	Pass	Pass	Pass

You lead your singleton club. Dummy wins with the ace and partner plays small. A low heart is led from dummy; partner follows with a small heart; and the queen forces out your ace. How can you reach partner's hand for a club ruff? Partner cannot have good clubs because he gave no encouragement. Besides, declarer probably would have finessed the ten or queen if he had nothing but little clubs. With a six card spade suit, a singleton small heart, and very little side strength, partner would not have doubled five hearts. He would have passed the decision around to you. With a weak five-card spade suit and ace-king-queen of diamonds, the double would look more tempting. So the best chance to get partner in is to lead a low spade. This is the only play that works since declarer's hand is

♠ Q   ♡ Q J 9 x x x x   ◇ —   ♣ K J x x.

NORTH
♠ A Q 9 2
♡ 8 4 3
◇ Q J 6
♣ K 5 3

EAST
♠ 10 7
♡ A Q J 5
◇ 10 9 8 5
♣ 9 7 2

Bidding

SOUTH	WEST	NORTH	EAST
1 ♣	Pass	1 ◇	Pass
1 ♠	Pass	3 ♠	Pass
4 ◇	Pass	5 ♠	Pass
6 ♠	Pass	Pass	Pass

Partner leads the six of hearts, and declarer drops the nine under your ace. Dummy's five-spade bid showed a good hand without heart control. Declarer bid six anyway, which means that he has heart control. Also, the spots in hearts indicate that partner led fourth best from a five-card suit and declarer dropped his singleton (although declarer could be hiding the deuce). With all of the indications that declarer has no more hearts, it would be a mistake to try to cash another heart unless a heart lead is completely safe. There are only two types of hands which declarer could have where a heart return would be costly:

♠ K x x x x   ♡ 9   ◇ K   ♣ A Q x x x x

and

♠ K x x x   ♡ 9   ◇ A x x   ♣ A Q J x x

The first hand is too unlikely to worry about, but the second is well within the realm of probabilities. A heart return gives declarer the entries for a dummy reversal, and he won't have to take the diamond finesse. The proper return is a diamond.

NORTH
♠ J 3
♡ J 8 5 2
◇ K J 7 3
♣ 10 7 5

EAST
♠ 10 9 7 6 4 2
♡ Q 9
◇ 9 2
♣ A J 6

East-West vulnerable,
match-point duplicate: bidding

SOUTH	WEST	NORTH	EAST
1 ◇	1 ♡	2 ◇	2 ♡
3 ◇	Double	Pass	Pass
Pass			

Declarer is an expert playing with his wife, which means that he would rather be playing the hand than defending. Partner leads the king of hearts and shifts to the king of spades. Declarer wins with the ace, pulls two rounds of trumps, and exits with a spade. Partner wins with the queen and leads a low heart to your queen, declarer dropping the ten. What should you return? If you lead the ace or a low club, it will cost a trick if declarer has Q x x. Leading the jack will save a trick if partner has K 9 8 x. Leading a spade may give declarer a sluff and ruff and, if his clubs are headed by the king instead of the queen, allow him to make his contract. But if partner had K Q x of spades, the ace-king of hearts, and the king or queen of clubs, why wouldn't he have made a takeout double rather than an overcall? Partner should have the doubleton king-queen of spades. If you trust your partner's bidding, a spade return must be safe. Declarer actually held

♠ A x x   ♡ x x   ◇ A Q 10 x x   ♣ Q 8 x.

CHAPTER III

Counting

DETERMINING the distribution of the unseen hands is known as counting. Two axioms form the basis for counting:

1. There are thirteen cards in each *suit*.
2. There are thirteen cards in each *hand*.

Thus if North, East, and South each has two spades, West must have seven. If West has seven spades, no hearts, and two diamonds, he must have four clubs. The process of counting is extremely easy—once you have the information to work with. Yet even experts sometimes fail to count a hand and make foolish mistakes as a consequence. In their case, the reasons are laziness and overconfidence. When a hand looks easy, they see no necessity for counting. My advice, based on bitter experience, is to count, or attempt to count, every hand.

As just stated, there is no difficulty in adding three sums and subtracting from thirteen. The problem is to determine what sums to add. In order to start counting, you need to know something about the distribution of one of the concealed hands. The surest way to obtain this information is for someone to fail to follow suit or "show out" when a suit is led. Suppose that you are the declarer. Dummy has four spades and you have five. When West discards on the second round of spades, you know that East started with three. Later in the play West discards on the third round of hearts. Since he started with a doubleton heart, you add his two hearts to the number you and dummy possess, and subtract from thirteen to find out how many East had. If you repeat the same process, playing diamonds until someone "shows out," you know the original distribution of the whole hand. It is unnecessary for anyone to "show out" of the fourth suit; you merely subtract the number of cards in three suits from thirteen.

Although a "show-out" gives you the only sure count of a suit, you normally cannot postpone your decision on how to play or defend a hand until there is a "show-out" in three suits. You might not obtain this positive information until trick eleven or twelve, and it would be too late to use it. The proper procedure is to draw inferences regarding the distribution of a suit from the bidding or play. You should form a tentative estimate of the distribution of all four hands based on the bidding and opening lead. As the play progresses, each trick should provide additional clues, confirming or disproving your original estimate. You must be willing to abandon your original estimate when the later clues prove it to be false.

NORTH
♠ A 10 9
♡ K Q J 8
◇ A 8 5 2
♣ K 7

SOUTH
♠ 8 6 4
♡ 9 7 5
◇ K Q 9
♣ A 10 4 3

Duplicate, North-South
vulnerable: bidding

EAST	SOUTH	WEST	NORTH
Pass	Pass	3 ♣	Double
Pass	3 NT	Pass	Pass
Pass			

West leads the queen of clubs, won by dummy's king while East plays a small club. You lead a diamond to the king and a low heart toward dummy, winning with the jack. A diamond to the queen is followed by another heart lead. West takes the ace, and exits with a diamond. East discards a spade while dummy's ace of diamonds wins the trick. On the third round of hearts West discards a club. What do you know about West's distribution? He has shown exactly two hearts and four diamonds. You know this for sure because an opponent showed out on the third round of each suit. West ought to have seven clubs for his three-club bid, but he cannot have seven since East followed to the first trick. He must have six clubs, which leaves him only one spade. So you cash the fourth round of hearts, the ace of spades, and throw him in with the fourth round of diamonds for a club return into your ace-ten. West's hand:

♠ Q ♡ A x ◊ J 10 x x ♣ Q J 9 8 x x

Actually there is an even better play, which is recommended against a very wild or tricky West player. After cashing the fourth heart, lead a club to the ace before cashing the ace of spades. If East shows out, as expected, lead a spade to the dummy and the fourth round of diamonds. This way you *know* West started with six clubs and one spade, and he still will have to let you make your ten of clubs. If East should follow to the second round of clubs, placing West with something like

♠ x x ♡ A x ◊ J 10 x x ♣ Q J 9 x x

you would know not to try for the end-play.

NORTH
♠ A J 9 2
♡ 3
◊ K 9 6 4 2
♣ A Q 8

Match-point duplicate: bidding

WEST	NORTH	EAST	SOUTH
3 ♡	Double	Pass	5 ◊
Pass	Pass	Pass	

SOUTH
♠ K 8 5
♡ 9 5 2
◊ A Q J 5 3
♣ 6 2

West leads the king of hearts and shifts to a trump. You win in your hand and ruff a heart with the king of diamonds, dropping East's ace. A diamond is led to your hand upon which East discards a club. You finesse the queen of clubs, which wins, followed by the ace and a ruff. West drops the king on the third round, and when you ruff your last heart, East discards another club. At this point, if you take time out to reconstruct West's hand you can determine his exact distribution. He started with seven hearts since East followed to only two rounds. West showed exactly two diamonds and three clubs. (East helpfully showed you that he had five clubs.) That leaves West with a singleton spade. If it is an honor, you have the rest of the tricks. When you cash dummy's ace, West drops the ten. Now you have a marked finesse through East's queen. West's hand was

♠ 10   ♡ K Q J x x x x   ◇ x x   ♣ K x x.*

NORTH
♠ 5
♡ K 10 7 4 3
◇ K 8 4 2
♣ K 9 6

Match-point duplicate,
both vulnerable: bidding

WEST	NORTH	EAST	SOUTH
1 ♠	Pass	Pass	2 ♡
2 ♠	4 ♡	Pass	Pass
Pass			

SOUTH
♠ 10 9 6
♡ A Q J 5 2
◇ J 3
♣ A J 8

West leads the king of spades and continues with a low spade at the second trick. Players often overlook clues such as this. Why did West lead low? If he were missing the queen, it would be a risky play to continue the suit at all, and he probably would exit with a trump. However, if he were missing the ace, he would be pretty sure his partner had it when the king held the first trick. His lead of a low spade was to prevent an honor clash and a ruffing finesse if his partner should hold the doubleton ace of spades, leaving you with 10 9 x x. Anyway, you ruff in dummy, East playing small, and return to your hand with a trump, to which both opponents follow. If East had A x x of spades and failed to keep the bidding open, he cannot have the queen of clubs. There are two possibilities for an over-trick—to play West for the doubleton queen, or to take a back-

---

* Declarer's play was, perhaps, correct at duplicate, but at rubber bridge he should have insured his contract by stripping the red suits and finessing the nine of spades rather than risking the club finesse.

ward finesse by leading the jack, and if covered by the queen, finesse the eight on the way back. You would rather know than guess what to do, and with careful preparation, you can get a count on the hand. The proper play now, because of entry problems, is to lead a low diamond toward the king. The king wins and a low diamond is returned. West wins your jack with the queen and leads another spade. You ruff in dummy again—high, just to be safe—and East's ace falls as expected. A diamond is led from dummy and ruffed while West's ace falls. Dropping the ace doesn't prove a thing, since the other diamond out is high, and either defender may have it. A trump is led to dummy, West discarding a spade, and dummy's last diamond is led and ruffed. West, who was false-carding with the ace, follows to the fourth round of diamonds. At this point, West's hand can be counted almost with certainty. One heart and four diamonds you are sure of, and he would not bid two spades, vulnerable, with

♠ K Q J x x ♡ x ♢ A Q 10 x ♣ Q x x

opposite a partner who could not keep the bidding open. Besides, that would leave East with A x x x of spades and a doubleton, with which holding he probably would not have passed one spade. West must have held six spades and only two clubs. Consequently the queen must fall. West's hand:

♠ K Q J x x x ♡ x ♢ A Q 10 x ♣ Q 10

NORTH
♠ Q 8 6 5
♡ 10 7
♢ A J 4
♣ K 8 5 4

East-West vulnerable: bidding

SOUTH	WEST	NORTH	EAST
1 ♠	2 ♡	3 ♠	Pass
4 ♠	Pass	Pass	Pass

SOUTH
♠ A K 9 7 3 2
♡ J 5
♢ K 10 6 3
♣ J

West leads the jack of spades. Let us analyze the bidding for a moment. North's three spade bid was a limit raise, which many experts use in competitive situations. However it is the defenders' bidding which is significant here. West made a vulnerable overcall, yet did not lead his suit. Apparently his heart suit is headed by a tenace, probably the ace-queen. You can see that he is also missing the jack and ten, and that he cannot have many high cards on the side. Considering all of these factors, he surely has at least a six-card suit. On the second trick, East discards a club on your high spade. On the third trick you lead the jack of clubs. West takes the ace and East plays the queen. West ponders a while. He knows his partner is solid in clubs but he is doubtful about the hearts. Probably influenced by East's failure to discard a small heart rather than a club at his first opportunity, West plays the ace and another heart to East's king. East exits with the ten of clubs, you win in dummy, discarding a diamond. When you ruff a club, West follows. Now it should be easy to figure out the opponents' distribution. West has shown two spades and three clubs. He cannot have the fourth club for two reasons. The nine has not been played, and East must have it; otherwise he could not have afforded to discard the queen and lead back the ten. Also, the first club discard was a clue that East held at least five. With only four, he would not discard one for fear of letting you establish dummy's fourth club. You can place West with an original holding of two spades, three clubs and six or seven hearts because of the bidding, which leaves him only one or two diamonds. This is as accurate a count as you need this time.

Sometimes when you are missing a queen, and you discover that one opponent has four of the suit and the other has two, you should play the hand with greater length for the queen as a percentage play. In this case, however, you do not need to worry about percentages since the contract is now a lay-down. Only East can have a diamond stopper and the good club. All the trumps should be led out, leaving the following ending:

NORTH
♠ —
♡ —
◇ A J
♣ 8

SOUTH
♠ —
♡ —
◇ K 10 6
♣ —

East must keep the nine of clubs to beat the eight—consequently only two diamonds. West had a maximum of two diamonds to start with. You play the ace of diamonds, lead the jack to the king, and the queen must fall. West's hand:

♠ J 10   ♡ A Q x x x x   ◇ Q x   ♣ A x x

NORTH
♠ K J 6
♡ K 8 7 6 3
◇ 6
♣ K 7 5 4

Match-point duplicate, neither side vulnerable: bidding

EAST	SOUTH	WEST	NORTH
1 ◇	2 ♡	2 ♠	4 ♡
Pass	Pass	4 ♠	Pass
Pass	5 ♡	Pass	Pass
Pass			

SOUTH
♠ —
♡ A Q J 9 4 2
◇ 8 7 4 3
♣ A 8 3

West leads the ace and another diamond, which you ruff in dummy. A heart is led to the jack, West discarding a spade, and a diamond is ruffed in dummy while West discards another spade. West has shown two diamonds and no hearts, but his black suit holdings must be determined by inference.

What could East have held for his opening bid? Six diamonds to the king-queen-jack, and perhaps the queen and jack of clubs. Surely he must have the ace of spades. If he had four spades to the ace and six diamonds, it is inconceivable that he would have failed to support spades somewhere along the line.

A low spade is led from dummy, and East plays small. If he had a doubleton ace, he probably would have played it rather than risk letting you make a singleton queen. He would figure that the ace would be ruffed out next round anyway, so why not play it immediately? With this clue, plus the fact that seven-card suits are more common than eight-card suits, it is logical to play East for an original holding of

♠ A x x   ♡ 10 x   ◇ K Q J x x x   ♣ Q x.

The exact club holding is uncertain. The important thing is that he should have only two clubs. Now the hand becomes a double-dummy problem. Ruff your last diamond; lead the king of spades, forcing East to cover. Then run all the trumps to squeeze West.

NORTH
♠ K 9 6 5
♡ 7
◇ K 9 6
♣ K Q 9 8 4

Match-point duplicate: bidding

WEST	NORTH	EAST	SOUTH
1 ♡	Double	Pass	3 NT
Pass	Pass	Pass	

SOUTH
♠ A 10 3
♡ A J 9 6 2
◇ Q 4
♣ J 6 2

The opening lead is the jack of diamonds, won by you with the queen. West has apparently led from ace-jack-ten of diamonds, and there is a strong likelihood that he has a two-suiter in hearts and diamonds. Consequently, you lead a low club rather than the jack to guard against the possibility that West has the singleton ace. West plays small, however, and the queen wins. Then a low club is led to the jack, forcing out the ace. West then cashes the ace of diamonds and leads another diamond. Almost surely he had five diamonds to start with to ac-

count for his persistence. Why didn't he duck a round of diamonds, saving his ace as entry in case his partner should win
a trick? Either he thought it unlikely that his partner would win
a trick or he was more afraid that you would end-play him for
an extra heart trick later if he were to play his diamonds that
way.

Now as you run dummy's club suit, West discards three
hearts. East follows to the third club, then discards a spade and
a heart. The fact that he discards one spade and no more is an
indication that he started with five. West must have started with
five hearts—otherwise how could he afford to discard three of
them? He also had five diamonds and two clubs, consequently
one spade. South has left A 10 3 of spades and A J of hearts.
Assuming that the inferential count is correct, East must have
four spades and one heart left. Dummy's king of spades is
played and everyone plays small. A low spade is led, and when
East plays small, you play the ten. It holds, and you score an
overtrick. Nor would it have done East any good to split his
spade honors. You would simply have cashed the ace of hearts
and exited with the ten of spades.

Players often lack the confidence to rely upon an inferential
count. In this case, declarer could rely upon it with a moral certainty. If West had started with Q x x x or K x x x of hearts,
aside from the fact that many players would not bid the suit,
he could not afford to discard three hearts after South's strong
jump in no-trump. There is no reasonable doubt about the number of hearts West started with. Since West "showed out" on the
third round of clubs, there is no doubt at all about the clubs.
You were sure that West had five diamonds from the fact that
he was so busy getting the suit established.

But suppose that you were wrong? It could not cost anything
to lose the lead to West if he had fewer than five diamonds to
begin with, and if he had the five diamonds you played him for,
it would not be possible for him to gain the lead.

NORTH

♠ A 7 5 4
♡ A 4 3
◊ 8 6
♣ K Q 9 6

SOUTH

♠ K Q 9
♡ K J 10 7 6
◊ A 10 5
♣ 4 3

West leads the jack of spades against your four-heart contract. You win with the king and lead a low club to the dummy.
West plays the eight, dummy the king, and East the ace. He
returns the queen of diamonds. You duck, win the diamond continuation, and ruff the third round. To your consternation, East
overruffs and returns a spade. West drops the ten under your
queen.

As was pointed out in the last chapter, if the opponents always knew what you had, they could toss their cards out at
random or false-card diabolically. But the fact is that they seldom
know exactly what you have, especially early in the play of the
hand. Most of the time they must give honest signals to avoid
working at cross purposes. When they lead a queen, they do
not have the king; when they show distribution by signaling,
they are giving an honest count.

In this case, West had six diamonds and probably two spades.
If he had J 10 x of spades originally, he could have dropped the
ten on the second round without costing a trick, whoever had
the nine, but it takes some effort to figure these things out. If
West played the ten immediately under your queen, it is fairly
safe to play him for only two spades. A heart is led to the ace,
and a low heart is returned with East playing small. The whole
hand now depends upon finding the queen. You have previously
decided that West had two spades and six diamonds.

Is there any clue to his club distribution? What club did he
play at trick two? Aha! You remember that he played a fairly

high spot! He wanted his partner to know how the clubs were distributed so that he would know whether to take the ace immediately or hold off. Perhaps this time he did not need to signal, but signaling of this sort is done by habit. Conceivably a signal in clubs could have given his partner a picture of the whole hand. Anyway, you decide to trust West's club signal as showing an even number of clubs, therefore a singleton heart. You take the heart finesse and it works!

The play of this hand actually took place as described, the declarer using the clues given by competent opponents rather than depending upon percentages alone.

The following hand is somewhat unusual because declarer is almost certain of the opponents' distribution at trick one and and is certain at trick two.

NORTH
♠ K 10 7 3
♡ 10 9 8 5
◇ J 6
♣ A Q 4

Bidding

EAST	SOUTH	WEST	NORTH
1 ♣	3 ◇	Double	Pass
Pass	Pass		

SOUTH
♠ J 8 4
♡ —
◇ A K 9 8 7 4 2
♣ 10 9 8

The opening lead is the deuce of clubs. When you play small from dummy, East wins with the king and returns the deuce of hearts. Upon ruffing, your first impulse is to take a safety play in diamonds by leading low to the jack. However, if West has all the diamonds, and if you misguess the spades or find both spade honors in the East hand, you may lose control. Also there is danger of a spade ruff. In other words, the "safety play" does not guarantee success and it is not even safe, although it surely is the right play if West has four diamonds.

Stop and count for a moment. West's lead of the deuce of clubs had to be a singleton or from a three- or four-card holding.

Since East played the king, it appears that the lead was from
J x x. That places East with, at most, four clubs. If East were
void in diamonds, he would have to hold a five card suit. He
would open one spade with five spades, four hearts and four
clubs, and he would probably open one heart or one spade with
4-5-0-4 distribution. The deuce of hearts return at trick two
definitely marks East with 4-4-1-4 distribution; he has no way of
knowing your problem and no reason to deceive his partner.
Consequently you lay down two high trumps and finesse the ten
of spades. West's hand:

♠ x x   ♡ A Q J x x   ◇ Q 10 x   ♣ J x x

Notice that if you had taken the "safety play" by leading a low
diamond at the third trick, West would have won the queen
and obtained the setting trick by means of a spade ruff.

There is a law of probabilities which is vital for you to
know and use. If the two unseen hands are denoted hand A and
hand B, the *probability* that a particular missing card will be
in hand A is the ratio of the number of cards of that suit in
hand A to the combined number of cards in that suit in hands
A and B. The *odds* that a particular card will be in hand A is
the ratio of the number of cards in that suit in hand A to the
number of cards in that suit in hand B. If you are missing the
queen of diamonds, for example, and if you know that West has
four diamonds to East's two, the odds are 4 to 2 or 2 to 1 (and
the probability 4/6) that West has the queen. Of course, if the
bidding shows that West cannot have the queen, you would
disregard this rule, which you apply when you have no other
clues.

There are many situations where you can use this rule of
probabilities. Suppose that your trump suit in a slam contract
is K Q 10 8 x x x opposite the singleton deuce. Assuming that
entries are no problem, should you take a first round finesse or
play for the jack to drop? You need a 3-2 break to hold the
losers to one, and if the suit does break 3-2, the odds are 3 to 2
that the jack will be in the hand with the three card length.
That means that the jack usually will not drop, while the finesse

is an even proposition. Consequently the finesse must be the right play.

There is another rule of probabilities that would sound even more formidable than the last one if I were to state it properly. Earlier I referred to having "room" in a hand for a certain card. If West has eight spades to East's two, West has five cards outside of spades to East's eleven. Common sense tells you that East is more likely than West to have any particular missing card outside of the spade suit. In fact the odds are 11 to 5. That is why you were advised, with nine trumps, to finesse for the queen rather than play for a drop when someone has shown a long suit. Even if West has only five spades to his partner's three, he only has eight chances (eight non-spades) to his partner's ten to hold your queen of trumps, so you have slight odds favoring a finesse through East.

NORTH

♠ A 10 7
♡ A J 5
♢ A 6 4
♣ K Q 7 3

Match-point duplicate: bidding

NORTH	EAST	SOUTH	WEST
1 NT	Pass	4 ♠	Pass
Pass	Pass		

SOUTH

♠ K Q 9 6 4 2
♡ K 10 7 3
♢ 8 5 2
♣ —

West leads the king of diamonds. You win with the ace and lead a *low* club. (East might play the ace if he has it without the jack.) But East plays small and you ruff. You play the king of spades, dropping East's jack, and a low spade to the ace, upon which East discards a club. The king of clubs is led and you discard a diamond. West wins with the ace and plays the queen and another diamond. East discards another club on the third round of diamonds while you ruff. You lead a trump to dummy's ten and cash the queen of clubs, discarding a heart. Both opponents follow to this club trick. At this point dummy has A J 5 of hearts and a small club. You have K 10 7 of hearts and the queen of trumps. You could get a complete count of the opponents' hands by ruffing dummy's last club with your last trump, but if you were then to finesse a heart into West and lose, he would be able to cash a diamond trick and defeat you. It is not necessary to get a complete count. West has shown three spades, five diamonds, and at least three clubs, leaving him two hearts at most to his partner's four. If you ruff dummy's last club and West follows, then the heart finesse will be a 100 per cent marked play after cashing dummy's ace. But suppose that West only had three clubs. The odds would still favor a heart finesse through East because of his greater length in hearts. Since you have enough information to know that you are going to finesse through East whether he has five hearts or four, there is no point in risking a set to get a more complete count.

The following hand occurred at the 1961 Summer National Tournament at Washington, D. C., and was played by my partner, Eddie Kantar. The bidding can be explained by the fact that this was a knock-out team of four; we were trailing by 26 I.M.P.'s at the half, and were "shooting" or gambling a bit at this stage.

NORTH
♠ A 5
♡ A K 7
◇ K Q 7 4
♣ A 9 8 6

SOUTH
♠ Q J 8 3
♡ Q 9 6 4 3
◇ A
♣ K Q 4

Bidding

SOUTH	WEST	NORTH	EAST
1 ♠	Pass	2 NT	Pass
3 ♡	Pass	4 ♣	Pass
4 ◇	Pass	7 ♡	Pass
Pass	Pass		

The opening lead was the ten of diamonds, won by the ace. A heart was led to the ace, and when neither the jack nor the ten fell, a low heart was led to the queen, followed by a heart back to the king. West discarded a diamond on the third round.

The king and queen of diamonds were cashed, South discarding spades and East dropping the jack on the third round. The problem was to take advantage of every possibility for the thirteenth trick before resorting to the spade finesse. A club was led to the king, dropping West's jack, and a club was led to the ace, West discarding a spade. Dummy's small diamond was then ruffed, leaving this position:

NORTH

♠ A 5
♡ —
♢ —
♣ 9 8

SOUTH

♠ Q J
♡ 9
♢ —
♣ Q

East is known to have two clubs and two spades. At this point the contract can be made whoever has the king of spades. If it is West, a simple finesse will work. If East has the king, the hand can be made by cashing the last trump and discarding a spade from dummy. If East discards a club, the queen of clubs will be cashed, establishing dummy's nine, and if East discards a spade, the ace of spades will be cashed, establishing declarer's queen. This line of play, known as a criss-cross squeeze, is far more artistic than simply taking a finesse. But Eddie counted the hands. West had shown five diamonds, two hearts, and a club—consequently five spades. Knowing that West had five spades to East's two, Eddie rejected the artistic play for the percentage play and simply took the spade finesse. West's hand:

♠ K x x x x   ♡ J x   ♢ 10 9 8 x x   ♣ J

NORTH
♠ A K 6
♡ 7 4 2
◇ J 7 6 4
♣ A Q 3

SOUTH
♠ Q J 10 8 3
♡ 9 6
◇ A 10 3
♣ K 10 5

Bidding

EAST	SOUTH	WEST	NORTH
Pass	Pass	Pass	1 ♣
Pass	1 ♠	Pass	2 ♠
Pass	4 ♠	Pass	Pass
Pass			

The opening lead is the queen of hearts. East overtakes with the king, cashes the ace, and leads the third round, upon which West plays small when you ruff. As I said before, the opponents could be doing something diabolical, but it looks as though West had a five-card suit. He should have the queen-jack-ten for his lead, and no one has played the jack or ten yet. Presumably West still has those cards. Trumps are played, and East discards a club on the third round, not looking very happy. The king and ace of clubs are cashed, ending in dummy. Everyone follows to each round. Now is the time to attack the diamond suit. With no clues whatever, you would have led low and put in the ten spot. This would hold the diamond losers to one if East had started with both the king and queen of diamonds or with the doubleton king or queen. However, it is extremely unlikely that East holds both the king and queen of diamonds because he has already turned up with a doubleton spade and the ace-king of hearts. Yet he neither opened the bidding nor competed over one club. Could East hold a doubleton honor in diamonds? Not unless all the clues are false. East started with two spades, since he showed out on the third round. He could not have held more than five clubs since West followed to two rounds. Probably he held four clubs, since with five he would not have been reluctant to discard a club on the third round of trumps. As pointed out before, the play of the heart suit indicates that East started with three. That leaves four diamonds in East's hand.

Even if he was coffee-housing over his discard on the third trump, he must still have three diamonds, so he could not have a doubleton honor. Consequently the proper diamond play is to lead the jack, playing *West* for a doubleton honor. East's actual hand:

♠ x x   ♡ A K x   ◇ Q x x x   ♣ J x x x

Defense

It is possible to be a reasonably good declarer without bothering to count the hands. You will misplay about one hand out of ten if you don't try to figure what the opponents have, but that could still be considered reasonably good. However, it is absolutely essential to attempt to count the unseen hands when you are defending. More points are chucked in this phase of the game than in any other. The effort of a little counting will often prevent a defensive blunder.

When the auction is over, before the opening lead is made, you should try to visualize the distribution of the opponents' hands from the bidding. If the bidding is

SOUTH	NORTH
1 ♠	2 ♠
4 ♠	

or

SOUTH	NORTH
1 NT	3 NT

you can form only a vague idea, but in other sequences you get quite an accurate picture. A good example is the hand from the last chapter where the bidding was

SOUTH	NORTH
1 ♠	1 NT
2 ♡	3 ♡
3 ♠	4 ♡

You were almost certain that declarer had 6-4-2-1 or 6-4-3-0 distribution before you made the opening lead. Every time a trick is played, especially when someone "shows out" of a suit, you should utilize the additional information to revise your estimate of the distribution.

NORTH
♠ A J 7 6
♡ K 5 3
◇ Q 8 6 5
♣ K 4

WEST
♠ 8 3
♡ Q J 10 6 2
◇ A K 3
♣ 10 6 2

Bidding

NORTH	EAST	SOUTH	WEST
1 ◇	Pass	1 ♠	Pass
2 ♠	Pass	4 ♠	Pass
Pass	Pass		

Your opening lead is the queen of hearts, which holds the trick. You continue with the jack, which declarer ruffs. He plays a spade to the ace and a spade back, with partner's queen losing to the king. This confirms the fact that declarer started with five spades. A club is led to the king followed by a club to declarer's ace. He then discards a diamond from dummy on the queen of clubs, ruffs a club in dummy, and ruffs dummy's last heart in his own hand. You should have been busy counting while all of this was happening so that when declarer leads a small diamond toward the dummy, you can duck without undue thought. Declarer has shown five spades, one heart, and four clubs. Since this leaves him three diamonds, you cannot lose by ducking. Declarer plays the eight from dummy, losing to partner's ten. Declarer's hand:

♠ K 10 x x x ♡ x ◇ J 9 x ♣ A Q x x

Declarer made it very easy for you to count his hand. If he had led the diamond several tricks ago, you would have been confronted with a guess. However, his line of play was reasonable. By stripping the side suits, he gave himself some additional chances.

NORTH
♠ A 10
♡ K 8 6 4
◇ K 10 6 3
♣ Q 10 5

EAST
♠ K 8 6 5 3
♡ 9 2
◇ 7 4
♣ A J 8 4

Bidding

SOUTH	WEST	NORTH	EAST
1 ♡	Pass	3 ♡	Pass
4 ♡	Pass	Pass	Pass

Partner's opening lead is the deuce of clubs. Dummy plays the ten and you win with the jack. You continue clubs, and declarer ruffs the third round. He then plays two rounds of trumps followed by the ace and another spade. You win with the king while declarer drops the queen. The only suit you know about with certainty is the club suit. A spade return cannot cost anything unless declarer has only two, so you should assume tentatively that he started with two. That leaves him nine cards in the red suits. Whether he has four hearts and five diamonds or five hearts and four diamonds, a sluff and ruff will not do declarer any good. You should lead a third spade. If declarer should happen to have another spade, the spade play will not help him, because it will not give him a sluff and ruff. If by some remote possibility, he should have another spade (and only three diamonds), a *club* lead would be costly since declarer would get rid of a losing diamond while ruffing in dummy. Declarer's actual hand:

♠ Q x ♡ A Q x x x ◇ A J x x ♣ x x

Obviously a diamond return would have enabled declarer to make the hand without guessing the location of the queen of diamonds.

```
                                    NORTH
                                    ♠ A Q 8 4
                                    ♡ 7 3
          WEST                      ◇ K 10 6
          ♠ 10 6 3                  ♣ 8 7 6 4
          ♡ Q 4
          ◇ A 7 3 2
          ♣ Q J 10 5
```

Bidding

SOUTH	WEST	NORTH	EAST
1 ♡	Pass	1 ♠	Pass
3 ♡	Pass	4 ♡	Pass
Pass	Pass		

It is usually bad tactics at duplicate and idiotic at rubber bridge not to take the setting trick when there is a chance to lose it. However, careful counting can show you when there is no risk. The opening lead is the queen of clubs, won by declarer's ace. He cashes the ace of hearts and finesses the queen of spades. Partner wins and returns a club. Declarer wins with the king and leads a spade to the ace. His next play is to finesse the jack of hearts, losing to your queen. You attempt to cash the jack of clubs, but partner ruffs your good trick with the ten of hearts and returns the jack of spades. Declarer ruffs and leads a low diamond. Declarer is definitely marked with two spades, six hearts, three clubs, and consequently two diamonds. Your proper play is to duck (fast!), and let partner win the ten with his queen. Declarer's hand:

♠ x x   ♡ A K J x x x   ◇ J x   ♣ A K x

Partner made the key play by ruffing your trick and returning a spade. If you had held the trick and had led a spade yourself, declarer would ruff, and if he led a diamond right away, you would not be sure whether he started with six trumps or seven. Or if you led the fourth round of clubs and partner ruffed, you would not know whether declarer started with three spades and one diamond or two spades and two diamonds. You would probably guess his distribution in either case, but you might not be quite certain enough to duck the setting trick. It is true that with a singleton diamond, declarer should have led it at trick two, but a good player would have led a diamond at trick two with the actual hand. It is dangerous to duck the setting trick, basing your play upon an inference, when declarer is a poor player.

<pre>
                          NORTH
                          ♠ 10 9 5
                          ♡ A 10 4 3
            WEST   ◊ 8 6 2
         ♠ K J 8 3   ♣ A Q 5
         ♡ Q 6
         ◊ K 9 7 5 4
         ♣ 8 3
</pre>

Match-point duplicate: bidding

SOUTH	WEST	NORTH	EAST
1 NT	Pass	3 NT	Pass
Pass	Pass		

Your opening lead is a small diamond, the jack forcing the queen. South cashes four club tricks while East follows suit. You and dummy discard diamonds. Declarer leads a heart to the ace and finesses the jack on the way back, losing to your queen.

Can you figure out declarer's distribution? He has shown four clubs. He must have the ace and ten of diamonds left, which means that he started with three. He surely has four hearts or he would have taken the heart finesse earlier rather than leave a good heart stranded in the dummy. This leaves only two spades in his hand. Now count his points. He had four in clubs, six in diamonds, and four in hearts, making a total of

14 outside of spades. His spade holding could be either Q x or
A x. If it is Q x, you can lead either the king or a low spade.
If it is A x, you must lead the king to save partner's queen and
avoid being end-played later. Therefore you lead the king to
guard against both possibilities. Declarer's hand:

♠ A x   ♡ K J x x   ◇ A Q 10   ♣ K J x x

NORTH
♠ K 9 8 4
♡ Q 8 5
◇ Q 8
♣ 8 7 6 3

WEST
♠ Q 6 3
♡ J 9 7 3
◇ J 7 6
♣ K Q 10

Bidding

SOUTH	WEST	NORTH	EAST
1 ♡	Pass	2 ♡	Pass
4 ♡	Pass	Pass	Pass

You lead the king of clubs and continue with the queen.
Declarer ruffs and plays the ace and a low heart to the queen.
To declarer's obvious disappointment, partner shows out on the
first heart lead, discarding a club. On the second trump he discards a diamond. A low spade is led to declarer's jack, and you
win with the queen. At this point you know that declarer had
six hearts and one club, consequently a total of six cards in
spades and diamonds. It is very tempting to make the "safe"
exit of a club, but if you think logically, you will realize that
what happens in spades from this point on is immaterial. Declarer is cold for his contract if he has A K x or A K x x of
diamonds, and he can't make the hand if he is missing the ace
or king of diamonds—unless you lead diamonds for him either
now or later. Your only safe exit is a spade. Declarer wins in his
hand, cashes the king of hearts, and leads another spade to the

king. When he leads the thirteenth spade, discarding a diamond, you ruff with your high trump and exit with the carefully preserved club. If you had led the club earlier, declarer would eventually put you on lead with your high trump, compelling you to return a diamond. Declarer's hand:

♠ A J x ♡ A K 10 x x x ◊ A 10 x ♣ x

	NORTH
	♠ 6 5 4
	♡ Q J 4
WEST	◊ K 9 7 4
♠ 10 9 8	♣ Q 8 3
♡ 8 7 5 2	
◊ A Q 10 3	
♣ 7 5	

Bidding

EAST	SOUTH	WEST	NORTH
1 ♠	3 ♣	Pass	3 ♠
Pass	4 ♣	Pass	Pass
Pass			

Your opening lead of the ten of spades is won by partner's king. He continues with the ace, and declarer ruffs. Partner obviously had A K Q J x x of spades and was trying to conceal his holding from the declarer, knowing that the situation would be clarified for you soon enough. Perhaps partner was hoping that you and declarer each had two spades, and that declarer would ruff low on the third round. Anyway declarer now leads a club to the queen (partner following) and plays the queen of hearts from dummy. When the queen holds, he ruffs a spade, cashes a high trump (partner discarding a spade) and the ace of hearts. He then leads a low diamond to the seven, and partner wins with the eight. He returns the king of hearts and declarer ruffs. What do you play when a low diamond is led toward dummy? You know by counting that declarer had 1-2-3-7

distribution. If he goes up with the king, he will make his contract. If he loses to partner, he will also make his contract, since
partner will have to give him a sluff and ruff. (It doesn't hurt
to count partner's hand too.) The only hope is to play the queen
so that if the king is not played from dummy you will be on lead
to cash the ace. Partner had the doubleton jack-eight of diamonds. An alert declarer would put up the king of diamonds
despite the false card in the spade suit. By ducking, he would
be playing you for Q J 10 x of diamonds, with which holding
you would have led the queen of diamonds in preference to a
tripleton spade. Even if partner should have the doubleton ace
of diamonds, he would then be end-played, so declarer has
nothing to lose by playing the king. Nevertheless, your correct
play is the queen of diamonds, since it is the only play that gives
declarer a chance to go wrong.

In some of these example hands, counting is a laborious process, and it is not till trick ten or eleven that you can determine
the exact distribution of the unseen hands. On a few occasions
you can tell almost with certainty at the first trick.

NORTH
♠ A Q 7
♡ J 8 6 3
◇ 7 2   EAST
♣ K J 8 3   ♠ K 8
                   ♡ 9 2
                   ◇ A 8 5
                   ♣ A 10 9 6 5 2

Bidding

SOUTH	WEST	NORTH	EAST
1 ♠	Pass	2 ♣	Pass
2 ♡	Pass	3 ♡	Pass
4 ♡	Pass	Pass	Pass

Partner leads the three of diamonds which you win with the
ace. The lead marks declarer with four diamonds. His heart
bids guarantee four hearts, and he almost surely has a five-card

spade suit since not many players would open a four-card spade suit headed by the jack. Consequently he should be void in clubs. It looks as though declarer will have to ruff diamonds in the dummy and if he can be persuaded to ruff clubs in his own hand, he may lose control. At trick two you return a low club! Declarer ruffs and takes the spade finesse. You lead another low club, and he ruffs again. When the queen of hearts fails to fall doubleton, he is a cooked goose because his hand is

♠ J 9 x x x   ♡ A K 10 x   ◇ K J 9 x   ♣ —.

	NORTH
	♠ Q 8 3
	♡ A J 8
WEST	◇ J 8 4
♠ J 7 5 2	♣ 9 7 4 3
♡ Q 6 5	
◇ 10 7 2	
♣ J 8 2	

Bidding

EAST	SOUTH	WEST	NORTH
1 ♣	1 ♡	Pass	2 ♡
Pass	3 ♡	Pass	Pass
Pass			

West leads the deuce of clubs which East wins with the ace. He returns the six and South plays the king, West the eight. At trick two West should be able to figure out the distribution of all hands! East obviously has a four card club suit and a maximum of two hearts. If he had 4-1-4-4 distribution, he would have opened the bidding one diamond, and if he had 3-2-4-4 distribution, he probably would still have opened the bidding one diamond. East should have 4-2-3-4 distribution, leaving South with 2-5-4-2 distribution. A heart is led to the ace at trick three, and West wins a heart finesse at trick four. A spade return runs the slight risk of declarer's holding the ace-ten doubleton; a diamond return is extremely dangerous, and a club lead may enable declarer to strip the hand for an end-play on partner. This is not a hand for aggressive action, so the best return is a heart. Declarer's hand:

♠ A 10   ♡ K 10 9 7 6   ◇ A 9 x x   ♣ K x

Sloppy defense would be costly this time since with any other return declarer would make his contract.

NORTH
♠ K J 9 6
♡ Q 10 4 3   *Bidding*
◇ K 8 4   EAST   SOUTH   NORTH
♣ 7 6   ♠ Q 10 7   1 ♡   2 ♡
                ♡ 8 5 2   3 ◇   4 ♡
                ◇ J 6
                ♣ A J 8 4 3

Partner leads the deuce of clubs. Declarer drops the ten under your ace and wins the club return with his king, partner playing the five. Declarer plays three rounds of trumps. Partner discards the nine of clubs on the third round. The way I play, West is marked with four clubs, since he would not lead small from 9 x x. Declarer continues with a diamond to the king and back to the ace while partner high-lows. A low spade is led to the jack, and you win with the queen. What should you return? Partner's high-low in diamonds shows that he started with an even number, which must be four in this case. Declarer's distribution is 3-4-4-2. A spade return would give up completely. A club return, giving declarer a sluff and ruff, is best. If declarer has a diamond loser, the sluff and ruff won't help him. He has to ruff something anyway, and there is only one trump left in each hand. In fact declarer undoubtedly does have a diamond loser; otherwise he would have cashed his diamonds before leading the spade to be sure of end-playing you. Declarer's hand:

♠ x x x   ♡ A K J x   ◇ A Q x x   ♣ K 10

Declarer ruffs in his own hand, discarding a spade from dummy.

Then he cashes the queen of diamonds. When the diamonds fail to split for him, he has to lead a spade and guess what to do.

Whenever declarer has a two-suiter with no more losers in the other two suits, it is usually a good defense to give him a sluff and ruff. It is better to make him ruff your suit which will not establish anything for him, than to let him ruff his own suit.

NORTH
♠ 10 4 2
♡ K J 6 4 3
◇ 9 8
♣ K 8 5

EAST
♠ K 6 3
♡ A 9 4
◇ 8
♣ A Q 10 9 6 3

Bidding

EAST	SOUTH	WEST	NORTH
1 ♣	1 ♠	Pass	Pass
2 ♣	3 ◇	Pass	3 ♠
Pass	4 ♠		

Partner leads the jack of clubs which holds the trick and he continues a club, which is ruffed by declarer. (Partner got off to a good lead with the jack of clubs rather than a low one. He figured there might be club strength in dummy, with a club shortage in declarer's hand.) Declarer plays the ace and king of diamonds. You ruff and return a third club, ruffed by declarer with the jack. He leads a heart to the jack, forcing out your ace. What do you return? Surely South has at least ten cards in spades and diamonds, so he cannot have any more losers in hearts and clubs. A sluff and ruff may force him to lose control of the hand, and it can't cost your side anything. Declarer's hand is

♠ A Q J 9 x ♡ x x ◇ A K J 10 9 ♣ x.

Wherever he ruffs, he is hopelessly in trouble. A passive return would permit him to make his contract with ease.

NORTH
♠ 10 9 5 2
♡ K J 8 6 4
♢ 9 5
♣ Q 8

EAST
♠ J 7 4
♡ Q 9
♢ K Q 9 6 4 3
♣ J 5

Bidding

SOUTH	WEST	NORTH	EAST
1 ♠	Double	2 ♠	3 ♢
4 ♠	5 ♢	Pass	Pass
5 ♠	Pass	Pass	Double
Pass	Pass	Pass	

Partner leads the ace of diamonds, which is ruffed by the declarer. He cashes the ace and king of spades, and partner discards a diamond on the second round. Declarer then leads the ten of hearts and lets it ride. What do you return upon winning with the queen?

First you must try to figure out South's distribution. You know that he had five spades and no diamonds. If he had only two hearts, his bidding would be rather strange, not to show clubs at all with six of them. Besides, with two hearts, he would surely have played the king, figuring your partner for the ace because of his take-out double. All the evidence points to declarer's holding at least three hearts—consequently five clubs. What about four hearts and four clubs? It is possible, but unlikely. Partner seems to have had a fairly skimpy take-out double, and it would have been very questionable indeed with only two hearts in his hand.

Assuming that declarer's distribution is 5-3-0-5, what should you return? A trump return is pointless since declarer can discard two clubs on the hearts and ruff one club. A club return is unnecessary because declarer cannot discard any "quick" club losers; if partner has the ace or king, it will eventually take a trick. A heart return will get you a ruff if partner has the ace (as is apparently the case) and cannot cost anything even if declarer has the ace. A diamond return cannot hurt if partner has the ace of hearts and a club trick since declarer can't ruff, pick up your trump, and knock out both of partner's winners without losing control. However, the heart return is the most straightforward play; it will save time and prevent partner from making an error.

If you are thinking and counting at all, you will not return a club or a spade. Declarer's actual hand was

♠ A K Q x x ♡ 10 x x ◇ — ♣ A 10 9 8 x.

CHAPTER IV

Help From Partner

IN THIS chapter we shall consider the partnership language, both the giving and receiving of information. We have not previously emphasized the help which partner can give us. After all, he is on our side and should be trying to help us solve our problems. However, we have many problems and he has to choose carefully what information to give us. We must trust him to give us the information which is most useful and must interpret his signals in that light. Suppose you lead the king of clubs and partner plays a high one. This can mean that he wants clubs continued; it can mean that he has club strength and hopes you will shift to a trump, to prevent declarer from ruffing his club losers; it can mean that since it is obvious clubs should not be continued, you should shift to the higher ranking side suit; it can mean that he has an even number of clubs and wants to show his distribution.

How can you tell what partner means? You must establish a priority of signals and use your common sense. Let's look at some examples. In each case, the bidding has been

OPENER	RESPONDER
1 ♠	2 ♠
4 ♠	

by the opponents. Your opening lead is the king of clubs, and partner plays the ten. The first dummy is

♠ Q 10 x x   ♡ A x x x   ◇ x x   ♣ x x x.

In this case, partner's high club calls for a continuation. He may have the ace (if you have led from K-Q); he may have the

queen (if you have led from A-K); he may have a doubleton
and is hoping that your lead is from ace-king so that he can
ruff the third round;* he may have nothing in clubs and nothing
else in his hand either, and he simply wants you to cash out
rather than shift. But his meaning is clear: Continue clubs!

The second dummy is

♠ Q x x   ♡ A x x x   ◇ x x x x x   ♣ x.

Now partner's message is not so clear. Conceivably he wants you
to continue clubs to make dummy ruff. More likely he is just
showing club strength and letting you use your judgment, which
means that you will shift to a trump to prevent declarer from
ruffing all of his club losers. You have to look at your own hand
and decide what line of defense is most promising. Perhaps you
should lead a red suit despite partner's signal, but the ten of
clubs surely does not suggest a shift to a heart or a diamond.

The third dummy is

♠ Q x x x x x   ♡ A x x   ◇ x x   ♣ x x.

If you have led from A K x x, it is very unlikely that partner
has a doubleton (placing declarer with five clubs). Partner
almost surely is showing you that he has the queen (but
definitely *not* the jack), and it is safe to underlead at the second
trick. The entire hand might be as follows, in which case the
underlead would be necessary.

---

* If the club lead is from A-K and partner has a doubleton, he should
encourage a continuation, but it can be disastrous to continue the suit
when the lead was from K-Q and declarer has A J x. Similarly if the lead
is from K-Q, partner should encourage a continuation with the jack, but
should not if your lead is from A-K. That's why Eddie Kantar and I
lead the ace from the ace-king.

NORTH
♠ Q 10 9 5 3 2
♡ A 8 5
◇ 8 3
♣ 8 2

WEST
♠ 7
♡ 6 4 2
◇ A 7 9 5 2
♣ A K 5 3

EAST
♠ 8
♡ 10 7 3
◇ Q J 10 4
♣ Q 10 9 7 4

SOUTH
♠ A K J 6 4
♡ K Q J 9
◇ K 6
♣ J 6

The fourth dummy is

♠ Q x x x x x   ♡ Q x x   ◇ Q x x   ♣ x.

This time it is hard to see how either a club continuation or a trump shift could do any good. It is obvious that a shift is called for, and partner's ten should be a suit-preference signal, asking for a heart shift.

If the contract were six spades and your opening lead were the king of clubs, what should a high club from partner mean when dummy has

♠ Q J x x   ♡ x x   ◇ A J x x   ♣ Q x x?

It should simply mean that he has an even number of clubs! He cannot possibly tell whether you should continue clubs or not because it depends upon how many you have. If the ace will hold, you ought to cash it. If not, you should shift—probably to a trump. Since partner cannot know whether you should attempt to cash your ace or not, the only intelligent signal is for him to show his distribution so that you will know what to do.

NORTH
♠ J 5
♡ A K 9
♢ K Q 8 6 2
♣ 9 7 2

EAST
♠ Q 10 8 6 4 2
♡ 8
♢ A J 10 7
♣ 8 5

Match-point duplicate: bidding

NORTH	EAST	SOUTH	WEST
1 ♢	1 ♠	2 ♡	Pass
3 ♡	Pass	4 ♡	

Partner leads the ace of spades. What card do you play? You should play the eight. It is true that partner's lead has probably cost a trick by establishing declarer's king. But there is no point in playing the deuce to show that you didn't like the lead (although I've seen many players do just that). Now that a spade has been led, a continuation cannot hurt, and a club shift could cost another trick. If you play low, partner would shift to a club. Declarer's hand:

♠ K 9 x   ♡ Q J x x x x   ♢ x   ♣ A Q x

In deciding whether to encourage a continuation, you should always consider what will happen if partner shifts. However most players are primarily influenced by what they have in the suit that partner leads. With three small, they play low to say they have nothing there, and let partner use his own judgment whether to shift or not. Roth and Stone tend to place the emphasis on whether they can stand a shift. Playing a deuce on partner's suit almost guarantees a high honor in the suit that he might shift to.

The difficulty is that the signal which may work best at trick two can mislead partner at trick three. Suppose partner leads the king of clubs and you have a complete Yarborough including the 8-5-2 of clubs. If you play the eight of clubs, you will prevent a shift, but when partner leads the second round of clubs, your five or deuce will mislead him. He will expect you to win the third round with the queen or by ruffing, and he may fail to cash another trick. It would be better to play the five the first time (not quite as clear a signal for a continuation) so that you could play the eight the next time and avoid an echo.

Another situation that causes confusion is this: Partner leads the king of clubs against a spade contract. Dummy has J x x x and you have Q x x. It would be nice for partner to underlead to your queen, but if you play your higher spot card, partner may think you have a doubleton. When he continues with the ace and another, declarer ruffs out your queen and establishes the jack. Consequently, unless it is vital to get two tricks and establishing the jack won't matter, or unless the bidding clearly indicates that you cannot have a doubleton, you should play small with this holding.

```
              NORTH
           ♠ K Q J 5
           ♡ 8 7 5
           ◊ Q 8 2                   EAST
           ♣ Q 9 6                ♠ 10 9
                                  ♡ A 3 2
                                  ◊ K 9 7
                                  ♣ J 10 7 5 3
```

Bidding

WEST	NORTH	EAST	SOUTH
1 ♣	Pass	2 ♣	2 ♡
Pass	Pass	3 ♣	Pass
Pass	3 ♡	Pass	Pass

The following hand illustrates that rather advanced reasoning may be required both to give and receive the proper signals. Partner leads the king of clubs. What is the best line of defense? If partner has A J 10 or A J 9 of diamonds, the right play might be to shift to the jack of diamonds before declarer could ditch his diamond losers on the spades. But let's analyze further.

If partner has three diamonds, that would leave declarer with four diamonds. In order for him to gain he would have to get *two* discards. He could only get two discards if he had A x of spades, which would leave partner with five spades. This is possible (the correct opening bid with

♠ 8 x x x x　♡ x　◇ A J 9　♣ A K x x

would be one club, the bad five-card spade suit being treated like a four-carder) but not very likely.

Suppose partner had four diamonds (headed by A J 9 or A J 10) and four spades. Then again a diamond shift would be right, but with 4-1-4-4 distribution partner surely would have bid one diamond instead of one club. So, while a diamond shift could conceivably be right, it is very unlikely to be necessary.

What about a spade shift? If partner's side strength is in diamonds, a spade shift probably will do no harm, and it may save a trick if partner's diamonds are headed by the ace-ten. If partner's side strength is the ace of spades, a shift to a low spade will enable you to get a ruff. Whatever you do, partner can see from the dummy that you have no tenace in spades and can only want a spade lead as a passive defense or to obtain a ruff. How can you ask for a spade shift? By playing the jack of clubs. Your club raises suggest a five-card length, and even if you had only four, you would hardly insist so violently upon a club continuation with the queen in the dummy. A shift is obvious enough so that the jack of clubs should be interpreted as a suit-preference signal.

Partner has

♠ A x x x　♡ x x　◇ J 9 x　♣ A K x x.

While it is possible from his point of view that you have a singleton spade, a doubleton is much more likely, in which case he must lead low to preserve his entry to give you a ruff. He has to guess whether you have one or two spades and can only be guided by probabilities. I have heard players say in situations like this that the jack of clubs should show a singleton, the ten show a doubleton, the lowest club ask for a diamond shift and an in-between club ask for a continuation. The trouble is that there are too many chances for errors when you play such a complicated system. Partner would probably assume that declarer had the jack if you were to play the ten, since you normally signal with the higher or highest of touching honors.

<pre>
                              NORTH
                              ♠ Q 10 9 7 6
                              ♡ K 5
              WEST   ◇ Q 10 8 6 3
        ♠ A 8   ♣ 5
        ♡ Q J 10 7 6 4
        ◇ K 9
        ♣ 7 3 2
</pre>

Match-point duplicate,
neither side vulnerable: bidding

SOUTH	WEST	NORTH	EAST
1 ♣	3 ♡	Double	5 ♡
5 ♠	Pass	Pass	Pass

The bidding is given as it actually took place in a hand from the 1961 regional tournament in San Francisco. All four players were strong and experienced. The three-heart bid should show less defensive strength and better distribution. West bid three hearts because it was late in the tournament and he felt like "shooting," or trying for an abnormal result. The double was the Roth-Stone negative double, asking opener to bid one of the unbid suits. The five heart bid was a pre-empt to compel opener to make his decision at the five level. Of course you would not bid three hearts with the West hand, but let us suppose that you were kibitzing during the auction. West has just received an emergency phone call and asks you to defend the hand for him.

Your opening lead is the queen of hearts. Dummy plays

small, partner plays the deuce, and declarer plays the nine. Try to decide how you would plan the entire defense before reading further.

With two small hearts in his hand, declarer probably would play the king from dummy. Quite likely he has a singleton, and for some reason prefers to have you remain on lead. The fact that partner played his lowest heart must mean that he wants you to shift—or that he can at least stand a shift. On the other hand, he could not know that you have only six hearts or that you have a trump trick. With trump control, the correct play is to continue a heart despite partner's deuce. If declarer has two hearts, you do not want him to discard the king of hearts on the ace-king of clubs. However, when you continue hearts, declarer ruffs and leads a low spade. You duck to allow for the remote possibility that partner has the singleton king. However, the queen wins, and another spade is led, with partner following suit.

This is the crucial point of the hand. Could partner's low heart at the first trick have been a suit-preference signal, calling for a club lead? No, because a club shift could not have been right at trick two, and it cannot be right now. It is impossible for partner to be void of clubs, and he cannot lose the ace if he has it. You should never interpret partner's signal as calling for an illogical play; his signal should guide you in choosing between *logical* alternatives. The low heart must have meant that he wanted you to shift to a diamond. Partner must have the ace of diamonds; otherwise it would be illogical for him to want a diamond lead. You must trust your partner and shift to a diamond in order to take the setting trick. If you don't take your diamond trick now, you will lose it, since declarer has

♠ K J x x   ♡ x   ◇ x   ♣ A K J x x x x.

He can get rid of dummy's entire diamond suit on the clubs!

Ironically, although partner intended his five heart bid as pre-empt, five hearts cannot be defeated. Partner's hand is

♠ x x   ♡ A x x x   ◇ A J 9 x x   ♣ Q 10.

NORTH
♠ 10 7 4
♡ A J 6 3 2
◊ K 5
♣ 8 6 3

WEST
♠ A Q 8 5 3
♡ 9 4
◊ J 8 4
♣ A K 7

Match-point duplicate,
North-South vulnerable: bidding

SOUTH	WEST	NORTH	EAST
1 ♡	1 ♠	2 ♡	Pass
Pass	Double	Pass	2 NT
Pass	3 ♣	3 ♡	Pass
Pass	Pass		

Your opening lead is the king of clubs. Partner plays the deuce, and declarer drops the queen. What should you play now? Partner surely has no more than two spades, so if you can get him in for a spade return, you should be able to take the ace and queen, and then give him a ruff. The first question is whether or not the queen of clubs is a singleton. If it is, then partner must have six clubs and five diamonds, for he would not have bid two no-trump, which obviously asked for a choice of minors in this sequence, with six clubs and only four diamonds. If partner had 1-1-5-6 or 2-0-5-6 distribution and either the ace of diamonds or the king of spades, he would have made another bid rather than sell out to three hearts. If declarer had a singleton club, the king of spades, and the ace of diamonds, he would have bid more strongly himself. The point in this analysis is that the queen of clubs is very unlikely to be a singleton, because if it were, either partner or declarer would have made another bid.

So the correct play is to cash the ace of clubs to see what signal partner will give. When you cash the ace, partner drops the ten, and declarer plays the jack. The ten must be a suit-preference signal—what else can it be? You shift to a low spade, and partner wins with the king and returns the suit. His hand:

♠ K x   ♡ x   ◇ 10 x x x x   ♣ 10 9 x x x

Failure to shift to a spade would allow declarer to make the contract by discarding one of dummy's spade losers on the queen of diamonds.

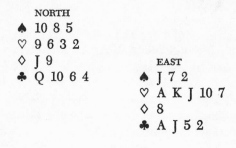

NORTH
♠ 10 8 5
♡ 9 6 3 2
◇ J 9
♣ Q 10 6 4

EAST
♠ J 7 2
♡ A K J 10 7
◇ 8
♣ A J 5 2

Bidding

EAST	SOUTH	WEST	NORTH
1 ♡	2 ◇	Double	Pass
Pass	Pass		

Partner leads a doubleton heart. You cash the king and ace, dropping declarer's queen on the second round. You then lead the ten rather than the jack as a suit-preference signal.

NORTH
♠ 9 7 4
♡ 10 8 3
◇ J 9
♣ Q 10 6 3 2

EAST
♠ J 7 2
♡ A K J 9 5 4
◇ 6
♣ A J 5

The bidding is the same as in the last example. The hands are almost the same, and the opening lead is the same. However, when declarer's queen of hearts falls on the second round, you have no choice but to lead the jack of hearts. This, obviously, cannot indicate a suit preference.

Suppose that the play continues as follows. South ruffs with the ten and partner discards a spade. A low diamond is led to the jack, and the nine of diamonds is led back, ducked to partner's king. What should you discard on this trick? The most clear-cut signal is the deuce of spades. Partner almost surely has a tenace holding in spades, and it is your duty to discourage a spade lead. His actual hand is

♠ K 10 x x x   ♡ x x   ◇ K 8 x x   ♣ K x.

Suppose that instead of J 7 2 your spades had been J 9 8. Now a discard of your "low" spade might look like encouragement.

With an expert partner, your proper play would be to discard your lowest heart. In this situation, where only you have hearts— consequently they being all of equal value—the discard of a low heart should show strength in clubs and the discard of a high heart should show strength in spades.

Which Card to Lead

Everyone knows that deciding which suit to lead, especially on opening leads, is often a problem, but most players assume that once you have decided which suit to lead, it is a cut and dried matter which card of that suit to lead. I do not share that view and would like to give you some of the factors which influence me.

Suppose that dummy has shown a very strong hand and partner has also shown a reasonably good hand, leaving very little for declarer and you (the opening leader). It may be important for you to lead through a tenace in dummy to take partner off an end-play, but you don't know what suit to lead. Rather than risk leading the wrong one, you decide to lead partner's suit with a holding of K x x x x. The correct lead would be the king to hold the lead so that you can make the proper switch, if necessary, after a look at the dummy. If you were to lead fourth best, partner would win the trick, and you might never again be on lead. Generally, however, with four or more cards of a suit, headed by an honor, you lead fourth best, and with three to an honor, you lead your smallest card.

With four or five small cards in the suit, you normally lead fourth best, since a count of the suit is usually the most important information you can give your partner. However, when you have strongly supported partner with four or five small cards, and partner already knows about your length, it is preferable to lead your top card, rather than fourth best, to deny an honor. The danger in leading low is that dummy will have K x or K x x, and partner will finesse the jack or ten, losing to declarer's singleton queen.

There are other combinations that partner will misplay if he thinks you have an honor. A similar situation arises even when you have not supported, but when dummy has bid no-trump, partner has over-called, and declarer ends up in a suit contract— probably with a singleton in partner's suit. In this situation where an honor is almost sure to be in dummy, you should lead your highest card, even if it is an honor. Suppose that dummy has K x x and partner has A J 10 x x x. If you lead low from Q x x, partner's ten will hold the trick, but he will be unable to continue the suit without establishing a trick for declarer. If you had led your top card you would remain on lead to continue the suit through the king.

With three small of a suit, it is generally of more value to partner for him to know that you have no high cards than it is to know that you have three. At least I think so. Consequently you should lead your top card. However, if you think partner might try to give you a ruff (when you have not supported the suit or shown a preference), you should lead low. This situation arises very seldom, on opening lead where you can anticipate partner's intentions to give you a ruff, but it occurs fairly frequently later in the play. One situation where it usually pays to lead low from three small on opening lead is when you have responded one no-trump to partner's opening major suit bid. If you lead your top card, he will probably assume that you have a doubleton.

When leading a suit partner has not bid, a lead of fourth

best should definitely guarantee that the suit is headed by an honor. This is particularly true against no-trump contracts, because it is important for partner to know whether you have the necessary high cards to establish the suit. Many of the top American players and most of the top European players agree. I also like a top card lead or next to top from four small or next to top card lead from five small against a suit contract, but this is a more controversial issue.

The problem of whether to show high cards or distribution can usually be solved on a logical basis during the middle of the hand.

The following hand was dealt in an international match.

	NORTH	
	♠ A 10 8	
	♡ Q 6 3	
	◊ A Q 5 3	
	♣ Q 4 2	

WEST		EAST
♠ 6 3		♠ —
♡ A K J 9 8		♡ 10 5 4
◊ K 6		◊ 9 8 7 4 2
♣ 9 8 7 6		♣ A K J 10 5

	SOUTH	
	♠ K Q J 9 7 5 4 2	
	♡ 7 2	
	◊ J 10	
	♣ 3	

Bidding

EAST	SOUTH	WEST	NORTH
1 ♣	1 ♠	2 ♡	3 ♠
Pass	4 ♠	Double	Pass
5 ♡	5 ♠	Pass	Pass
Pass			

Over East's semi-psychic opening bid, an immediate four-spade overcall would have made both the bidding and defense quite difficult for East-West. West led the king of hearts and shifted to the nine of clubs. East tried to cash a second club, but South ruffed and eventually got rid of his heart loser on the diamonds. It should be obvious to West that the most important thing to show was his distribution, so that his partner would know how to cash out. Consequently he should have led the six of clubs in an effort to show four, even though the nine of clubs would be the right lead in some other situation.

NORTH
♠ 10 5
♡ 8 6 5 3
◇ A K 7
♣ A Q J 4

EAST
♠ J 8 3 2
♡ J 10 9 2
◇ 6 2
♣ K 7 3

Bidding

WEST	NORTH	EAST	SOUTH
1 ♠	Double	2 ♠	5 ◇
Pass	Pass	Pass	Pass

Partner leads the king of spades, won by declarer's ace. Declarer immediately finesses the jack of clubs. Since declarer has an obvious trump entry to repeat the club finesse, there is no point in ducking. When you win, you see a probable discard coming up in the club suit and you would like to cash out your major suit winners. If partner had six spades to start with and A Q x of hearts, he will need a heart lead by you. Whatever he has, a heart lead can hardly be wrong, but which heart should you lead? Normally you would lead the jack, top of a sequence. In this case the fact that you have a sequence headed by the jack is completely immaterial; the important thing is that you have four. You should lead the deuce so that when declarer plays the king, partner will know what major suit winner to cash. If his hand is

♠ K Q 10 x x x   ♡ A Q x   ◇ x   ♣ x x x

he will cash the heart winner; if his hand is

♠ K Q 10 x x   ♡ A Q x x   ◇ x   ♣ x x x

he will cash the queen of spades. If you had led the jack, partner might try to cash the ace of hearts with the latter hand. As a corollary, it is obvious that with three hearts (J 9 2) you should lead the jack, not the deuce. We mentioned earlier that you sometimes lead low from three small to differentiate between three small and two small. In this case, the crucial holdings are four and three hearts, and you must differentiate between those holdings.

The example just given is not easy to understand. The important thing is to visualize partner's hand and his problem. Usually there are two significantly different holdings you might have. When you realize what his problem will be, you can find a way of showing which of these holdings you have.

	NORTH		
	♠ K J 8	*Bidding*	
	♡ 9 5	SOUTH	NORTH
WEST	◇ K Q J 6 2	1 ♠	2 ◇
♠ 9 4	♣ 8 5 3	2 ♠	3 ♠
♡ A 10 8 7		4 ♠	
◇ A 5			
♣ K 10 7 4 2			

Your opening lead is the fourth best club. Partner's queen drives out the ace. Declarer pulls two rounds of trumps and knocks out your ace of diamonds. The problem, obviously, is in what order to cash the setting tricks in hearts and clubs. Partner's play to the first club trick indicates that declarer has the jack. If it is alone, you must be able to cash two heart tricks to defeat the contract. That will require finding partner with the king of hearts. If declarer has the J x of clubs left, you need to get partner in with a heart for a club return. In either case, he has to have the king of hearts, so you lead a low heart.

Now let's move over to partner's seat and look at the problem from his point of view. Suppose that he has

♠ 10 x   ♡ K Q J x x x   ◇ x x x   ♣ Q x.

He doesn't know your heart length for sure (you would have

led low for the same reason from A x x of hearts and A x x of diamonds). However, he knows that you do not have more than five clubs since the only spot lower than the four, which you led, is the deuce. (Besides, with six clubs you would have no problem deciding how to cash out.) Consequently the club return must be right. If you have the king-ten you will cash them. If your clubs are worse—king-nine perhaps—you will see that another club cannot be cashed and you will try a heart. If partner had

♠ 10 x ♡ K x x x x ◇ x x x ♣ Q x x

he will return a heart. By your lead of the deuce he can tell that one more heart is cashable. Then you can lay down your king of clubs. I realize that the reasoning necessary for this sort of hand is complicated and not easy to explain. Try giving the players various distributions and work out what they should do in each case to be sure of cashing all of their winners. The two critical hands for declarer are

♠ A Q x x x x ♡ x ◇ 10 x x ♣ A J x

and

♠ A Q x x x x ♡ Q J ◇ 10 x x ♣ A J

(exact heart holding immaterial). When declarer has two heart losers and A J x of clubs you will always defeat him. The second setting trick is unimportant. There are many situations in which the defender who has an accurate count of the hands should "take charge" of the defense rather than give his partner an opportunity to make a mistake. A spectacular example of this is the following:

NORTH
♠ Q 7
♡ 2
◊ A J 10 9
♣ 9 8 6 4 3 2

EAST
♠ K 9 6
♡ J 4 3
◊ Q 8 5 4
♣ Q 7 5

Bidding

SOUTH	WEST	NORTH	EAST
1 ♣	Pass	1 ◊	Pass
1 ♡	Pass	2 ♣	Pass
3 NT	Pass	Pass	Pass

Who would ever suspect that you could make the star play with the dull-looking East hand? Partner leads the deuce of spades, covered by the queen, king and ace. Declarer leads the ace of clubs upon which partner discards a heart, the king of clubs upon which partner discards a diamond, and the jack of clubs upon which partner discards another diamond. What do you return upon winning with the queen? The bidding, the opening lead, and partner's discards all clearly show that declarer started with 4-4-1-4 distribution. It is too much to hope that a spade lead will enable partner to cash four tricks. A much more promising defense is to knock out dummy's diamond entry before declarer can unblock the club suit. The obvious lead is a small diamond, and that would be the correct lead against the average declarer. But suppose when partner plays the king of diamonds, he is allowed to hold the trick? It is easy for you to count the declarer's distribution, but partner will not be able to count it, since he doesn't know whether you started with four spades and three diamonds or three spades and four diamonds. In either case, your correct play would be the same—to lead a diamond before the club suit could be unblocked. So rather than risk declarer's ducking the diamond with a singleton, and partner's continuing the suit, you should return the queen of diamonds! Partner will have to duck, and if declarer does likewise, you will shift back to spades. The message would be clear: "Declarer has no more diamonds." Leading the queen runs the risk that declarer's singleton diamond is the king, but it avoids a guessing situation in all other cases.

A more clear-cut example of "taking charge" is the following:

```
                NORTH
             ♠ 8 4 2
             ♡ A Q 5
             ◇ K Q J 8          EAST
             ♣ J 5 2         ♠ K Q 10 5
                             ♡ 6 4
                             ◇ 9 5
                             ♣ A 10 9 7 4
```

Bidding

NORTH	EAST	SOUTH	WEST
1 ◇	1 ♠	2 ♡	3 ♠
Pass	Pass	4 ♡	Pass
Pass	4 ♠	Pass	Pass
5 ♡	Pass	Pass	Pass

Partner leads the three of spades, and declarer wins with the ace. He cashes two trumps, partner discarding a spade on the second round. Declarer then leads the ten of diamonds and continues diamonds. Partner wins the third round with the ace while you discard a low club. Partner leads the king of clubs. You know that declarer has a spade left since partner's lead showed a maximum of four spades. Rather than leave anything to chance, you should overtake partner's king of clubs and cash the king of spades. In fact, failure to do so would be sheer boobery. When you know what to do, do it! Declarer's hand:

♠ A x   ♡ K J 10 x x x x   ◇ 10 x x   ♣ x

NORTH
♠ 5
♡ K Q 9 8 5 4
◇ A 8
♣ K J 9 6

EAST
♠ 9 7
♡ J 7 5
◇ K Q 10 4
♣ Q 8 7 5

Bidding

NORTH	EAST	SOUTH	WEST
1 ♡	Pass	2 ♠	Pass
3 ♡	Pass	4 NT	Pass
5 ◇	Pass	5 ♠	Pass
Pass	Pass		

Partner leads the deuce of diamonds, which is won by dummy's ace. Declarer then cashes three high trumps, partner discarding a club on the second round and a heart next time. Declarer must have started with nine spades and at least three diamonds, as indicated by partner's opening lead. If his thirteenth card is a small heart, nothing can go wrong since partner would not duck a heart lead. If declarer's thirteenth card is a small club, partner might duck because he does not know declarer's diamond distribution, and from his point of view, the right play might be to give declarer a guess in the club suit. You do not want partner to duck, so the proper play is to discard the queen of clubs. Now he would have no reason to duck a club.

It might be noted that declarer committed a serious error in bidding Blackwood with a void, and he made a more serious error in winning the opening lead. Partner will reason declarer would not bid or play the hand this way with his actual holding, which is all the more reason to give partner a message in this spectacular fashion. Although declarer may have misplayed (and misbid) the hand, your job is to take advantage of the situation as it exists—not to point out how declarer could have made the hand anyway. As was pointed out before, good bridge consists partially of capitalizing on the opponents' mistakes.

So many examples have been given of leading to show distribution you may get the impression that I think showing distribution is more important than showing high-card strength. That is far from the truth. The opening leads I recommend are designed primarily to show where the high cards are, only secondarily to show distribution. In signaling, the primary duty is to show the presence or absence of high cards in the suit. It is the exceptional case—usually in cash-out situations—where it is necessary to show distribution instead. Suppose for example, that you lead the queen of hearts (partner having bid the suit) against a spade contract.

NORTH
♠ K J 6
♡ 9 5
◇ Q J 7 5 2
♣ A Q 6

WEST
♠ 9 7
♡ Q J 7 3
◇ K 4 3
♣ 9 7 5 2

Partner plays the deuce and your queen holds the trick. Obviously partner wants a club switch. Your correct lead is the nine of clubs. If partner has K 10 x, you do not want him to duck if declarer plays small from dummy. If he ducks with that holding, you may never get a club trick. The number of clubs you have is unimportant. Suppose partner has the K J x, or K J x x. If dummy ducks completely, partner will win with the jack and underlead his ace-king of hearts for another club lead. He can afford the underlead since your opening lead indicated that you held the jack, which illustrates the general rule that it is better to show high cards than to show distribution. Whatever declarer has, no cashable tricks will be lost. On the other hand, if partner had K 10 x of clubs and you had J x x or J x x x, you would hate to have partner play the king if a clever declarer should duck in dummy. Therefore, to avoid a defensive error you should lead low from the jack, but high otherwise. Now partner cannot go wrong.

```
              NORTH
          ♠ Q 10 5 2
          ♡ 7 3
          ◇ A 9 4              EAST
          ♣ K Q J 8         ♠ 6 3
                            ♡ Q 8 5 2
                            ◇ K 8 2
                            ♣ 9 7 4 3
```

Bidding

NORTH	EAST	SOUTH	WEST
1 ♣	Pass	1 ♠	Pass
2 ♠	Pass	4 ♠	Pass
Pass	Pass		

Partner leads the queen of diamonds, won by dummy's ace. You should play the eight to encourage a diamond continuation when partner regains the lead. This is the general rule, based on common sense. Suppose that dummy's diamond holding were A 10 x. If declarer had the king, he would almost surely win in his hand so as to preserve a tenace over partner's jack. Consequently when he wins with the ace in dummy, you are almost marked with the king. With a thinking partner, you should play the deuce to show your distribution since he already knows about your king from declarer's play. In this case, ironically, the deuce would be more encouraging than the eight. If partner's hand is

♠ x   ♡ A J x x   ◇ Q J 9 x x   ♣ A x x

he will lead a small diamond upon winning the ace of clubs, and you will return a heart. If he has

♠ K x   ♡ J x x x   ◇ Q J 9 x   ♣ A x x

he will cash the jack of diamonds before leading low to your
king. By your showing your distribution, partner knows how
many diamond tricks can be cashed.

When defending against any contract, suit or no-trump, the
standard discard from a sequence headed by a jack or better is
the top card. If you discard a king, you deny possession of the
ace; if you discard a jack, you deny possession of the queen.
Suppose that partner leads a small card at no-trump and dummy
plays the king. With Q J x, you would play the queen. Partner
must have an honor, either the ace or ten, to lead small, and in
either case you want him to know it is safe for him to continue
the suit. With J 10 x, you would play the jack. The ten would
guarantee the queen since you would not bother to show 10 9 x.
Occasionally you may fail to signal because you think it is necessary to retain both honors, but if you can afford an honor, play
the higher one. It was not recommended that you play the ten
from 10 9 x, since it is more important to guarantee a higher
honor by the play of the ten. However, if partner knows whether
you have a higher honor from the way a hand is played, the
ten would be the right play from 10 9 x or K 10 9 x, and discarding the nine would deny possession of the ten. This explana-
tion is necessary to appreciate fully the defense of the following
hand.

```
                              NORTH
                            ♠ Q 7 5 3
                            ♡ Q 10 8 4
              WEST          ◇ J
            ♠ 8 6           ♣ 8 6 4 3
            ♡ A K 9 6
            ◇ 8 5 3
            ♣ A J 10 9
```

North-South vulnerable: bidding

SOUTH	WEST	NORTH	EAST
1 NT	Pass	Pass	Pass

On opening lead, you have a tough decision. Should you be

aggressive or passive? You decide to be passive and try for all four club tricks. Logical or otherwise, your opening lead is the eight of spades. Partner plays the deuce and declarer wins with the jack. He then leads a low heart won by dummy's ten when you duck. A heart is led back. You win and cash the other high heart to see what partner will discard. He discards the nine of spades. Under these circumstances, the discard of the nine positively denies possession of the ten. The fact that partner played the deuce the first time plus the fact that he is discarding a spade shows that he does not want any more spade leads. Declarer surely started with A J 10 and partner had K 9 7 2. With two or three low clubs, partner would discard a club to prevent you from leading one, so the fact that he has not discarded a club is encouraging. It makes you feel good that you did not lead a club originally since partner's club honor is probably the queen. You lead the eight of diamonds covered by the king and ace. Declarer plays the queen and another diamond for down three. He could have done better, of course. His hand:

♠ A J 10   ♡ J x x   ◇ A Q x x   ♣ K x x

Some of the most interesting hands in which partnership information is given or received do not involve signals at all. Each partner trusts the other to reason logically and inferences are drawn from the line of play adopted. For example:

NORTH
♠ A Q 4 2
♡ A Q 5
◇ 6 3
♣ A Q 10 3

EAST
♠ 9 7 3
♡ 4 2
◇ A K 10 5
♣ K J 6 5

Bidding

NORTH	EAST	SOUTH	WEST
1 ♣	Pass	1 ♠	Pass
4 ♠	Pass	Pass	Pass

Partner leads the queen of diamonds upon which you play the five spot, hoping that he can tell from his hand that you want a club switch. Sure enough, he leads the seven of clubs. Dummy plays small and you win with the jack. You now lead the ten of diamonds so that partner can overtake with the jack and lead another club. It is very obvious what you want partner to do. But your ten of diamonds holds the trick! It should not be hard to figure out that partner has no more clubs when he fails to overtake your diamond. Consequently you should give him a club ruff since it cannot lose to do so, and you may still get your king later. Declarer's hand:

♠ K J 9 x x   ♡ x x   ◇ x x   ♣ 9 8 x x

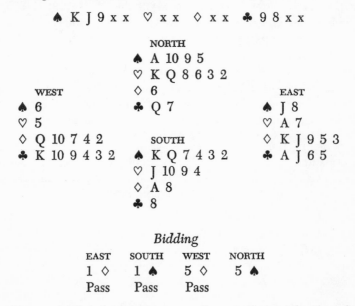

```
                       NORTH
                       ♠ A 10 9 5
                       ♡ K Q 8 6 3 2
     WEST              ◇ 6                    EAST
     ♠ 6               ♣ Q 7                  ♠ J 8
     ♡ 5                                      ♡ A 7
     ◇ Q 10 7 4 2      SOUTH                  ◇ K J 9 5 3
     ♣ K 10 9 4 3 2    ♠ K Q 7 4 3 2          ♣ A J 6 5
                       ♡ J 10 9 4
                       ◇ A 8
                       ♣ 8
```

Bidding

EAST	SOUTH	WEST	NORTH
1 ◇	1 ♠	5 ◇	5 ♠
Pass	Pass	Pass	

Partner leads a heart—almost surely a singleton. The thoughtless play is to give him an immediate ruff. The flaw is that he won't know what to return and would probably return a diamond since that is the suit you have bid. The correct play is to cash the ace of clubs. Partner plays small since he wants a heart ruff. If by any chance he has led a doubleton heart, he would encourage a club continuation with his ten. After cashing the ace of clubs, you give partner his heart ruff and he attempts to cash the king of clubs. As it happens, declarer ruffs, but at least the contract is set.

NORTH
♠ K J 10 8 4
♡ 7 6 2
◇ 3
♣ Q 8 5 3

EAST
♠ 9 7
♡ A 10 8 3
◇ Q 5 2
♣ K J 7 6

Bidding

SOUTH	WEST	NORTH	EAST
1 NT	Pass	2 ♣	Pass
2 ♡	Pass	2 ♠	Pass
2 NT	Pass	Pass	Pass

Partner leads the seven of diamonds. You win with the queen, declarer dropping the eight. You return the five, declarer plays the ten and partner wins with the jack. He returns the six and declarer takes his ace. All appearances indicate that partner had a six card suit since declarer could hardly afford to play the eight on the first round with A 10 8 3. Declarer then adopts the following peculiar line of play. He plays a low club, covering partner's ten with the queen. You win and return a low heart, won by declarer's king. He plays the ace of spades, finesses the ten, and cashes the king. You and declarer each discard a heart. Declarer then cashes the ace of clubs and gives you a club trick. Partner discards two diamonds on the clubs. At this point you have a perfect count on the hand. Partner started with four spades, six diamonds, two hearts and a club. He still has his second heart, the good queen of spades and a good diamond. If his heart is the jack, you should toss declarer in with the club to make him lead away from his Q x of hearts. If partner's remaining heart is the queen, you should lead a low heart so as to take the rest of the tricks. However, the correct play is not a

matter of guesswork. Partner's heart must be the queen. If he
had the jack of hearts instead, he should have thrown it away
on the previous trick to prevent you from underleading.

For a change, in the next two examples, we shall show all
four hands. In both cases something went wrong with the defense. See if you can spot the errors.

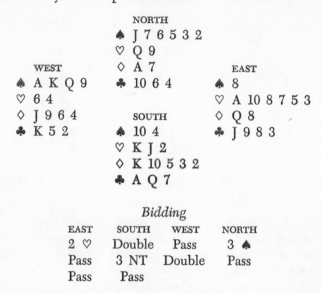

NORTH
♠ J 7 6 5 3 2
♡ Q 9
◇ A 7
♣ 10 6 4

WEST
♠ A K Q 9
♡ 6 4
◇ J 9 6 4
♣ K 5 2

EAST
♠ 8
♡ A 10 8 7 5 3
◇ Q 8
♣ J 9 8 3

SOUTH
♠ 10 4
♡ K J 2
◇ K 10 5 3 2
♣ A Q 7

Bidding

EAST	SOUTH	WEST	NORTH
2 ♡	Double	Pass	3 ♠
Pass	3 NT	Double	Pass
Pass	Pass		

I shall point out at the start that the only person who had
his bid was West, but it is defensive errors that you are sup-
posed to look for. West led his top heart, ducked by East. The
ace, king and another diamond were played. East followed with
a lower heart than he had played at the first trick. West led his
other heart and East returned a spade. West was then end-
played and the contract was defeated only two tricks. On a
double-dummy basis East was at fault; he could have returned
a club rather than a spade. On any sort of rational basis West
was clearly at fault. Once the dummy was depleted of entries,
why didn't West cash his high spades to prevent a spade return?
If he didn't want to cash all three, he could have led at least

two rounds—or one round by cashing the queen. From East's point of view, West had to have a spade holding he could not lead from—probably K Q 10 x.

Perhaps you do not consider it a tragedy to score 300 instead of 500 on what should have been a part-score hand. Bad defense was more costly in the next example.

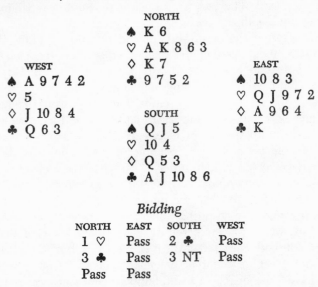

NORTH
♠ K 6
♡ A K 8 6 3
♦ K 7
♣ 9 7 5 2

WEST
♠ A 9 7 4 2
♡ 5
♦ J 10 8 4
♣ Q 6 3

EAST
♠ 10 8 3
♡ Q J 9 7 2
♦ A 9 6 4
♣ K

SOUTH
♠ Q J 5
♡ 10 4
♦ Q 5 3
♣ A J 10 8 6

Bidding

NORTH	EAST	SOUTH	WEST
1 ♡	Pass	2 ♣	Pass
3 ♣	Pass	3 NT	Pass
Pass	Pass		

West led the four of spades, upon which the king, eight and five were played. A club was led to the ace, and the jack of clubs continued. West went right in with the queen and returned the jack of diamonds. Dummy played small, but East won the ace and returned a spade. Declarer then scored ten tricks. Let's listen to the comments.

WEST: "Why hit the panic button? What was that ace-of-diamonds play for?"

EAST: "I thought they had nine tricks if I ducked—five club tricks, two heart tricks, a spade and a diamond. My only chance to beat the hand was to find you with five spades to the ace-jack."

"If my spades were ready to run, and if I didn't want you to duck the diamond, I wouldn't have led the jack. I'd have led the eight or something like that."

"You couldn't be sure the spades would run, even if you had A J x x x since I might have just had two."

"Yes, but I would have played you for three if necessary to beat the hand. The jack of diamonds meant I was willing for you to duck with the ace."

As is often the case, both defenders were at fault. West's comment about leading a diamond other than the jack if he wanted East to step right in with the ace is logical. However, West could have made things much easier for his partner by ducking the second round of clubs. Then East would know that declarer only had four club tricks, and he would have no excuse to hop up with the ace of diamonds. The principle is that you should hold off as long as possible, if you know that declarer must develop the suit, in order to give partner a count.

As declarer you hold A J 10 9 x x opposite four small, and the ace catches the king or queen. What do you play to the second round? No, I am not joking. The correct play is to lead the jack. Many players carelessly lead small, knowing that the remaining high card, whatever it is, must fall. But why make the situation clear to the other defender? Make him guess whether you have a five or six card suit. Suppose your suit were A J 9 8 x opposite four small, and again the king or queen comes up on your right. It would be desirable to go to dummy to lead toward your J 9 8 x, but we shall assume that you do not have an entry or cannot afford to use an entry. If you must lead a card from your hand, again you should lead the jack. If West wins with the queen, East won't know whether his partner is out of the suit, whether he still has a small card, or has another winner. If you lead small, allowing the ten to win, it is easy for him to read the whole suit.

NORTH
♠ A K J 7 4
♡ Q J 6 3
◇ J 8 6
♣ 7

EAST
♠ 10 6 3 2
♡ 9 8
◇ K Q
♣ A 9 8 5 2

Bidding

SOUTH	WEST	NORTH	EAST
1 ♡	Pass	1 ♠	Pass
2 ♡	Pass	4 ♡	Pass
Pass	Pass		

Partner's opening lead is the four of clubs, won by your ace. The only chance to set the contract is to find partner with the ace of diamonds. If you cash the king and queen, partner will signal encouragement, waiting for you to lead the third round. By playing your diamonds in abnormal order—the queen first and then the king—partner will realize that you are trying to convey a message to him, and it won't be hard to figure out what the message is.

NORTH
♠ A Q 5
♡ 7 3
◇ K 8 6 3
♣ A K 10 3

EAST
♠ 9 6
♡ A Q
◇ Q 9 7
♣ J 9 7 5 2

Bidding

WEST	NORTH	EAST	SOUTH
3 ♡	Double	Pass	4 ♠
Pass	Pass	Pass	

Partner leads the deuce of hearts, and you win with the ace. Do you really think partner pre-empted with a four-card suit? Of course not. His lead of the lowest card—rather than the normal fourth best—means he wants to ruff something. His most likely void is in clubs. At this point you are sorry you did not play the queen of hearts to win the first trick. Maybe you can still recover by returning the jack of clubs. Partner ruffs, as expected, and seeing your violent suit preference, he returns another low heart to your queen for another club ruff. The moral of these last two examples is clear. When you deviate from the normal, you should always have a reason so that partner can draw inferences from your play. If you cash honors in random order or lead your seventh best card just to be fancy, your partner will be unable to believe you when you really want to give him a message.

Suppose you are the East player, defending against a suit contract. You want partner on lead very badly for some reason. Dummy has x x of your good suit, and you have A K Q x x. Your proper lead is the queen. When declarer fails to cover, partner will realize what your holding is, and he will give you encouragement if he has the jack. If your suit were A K Q J x, you would lead the jack so that partner would signal with the ten.

```
            NORTH
        ♠ K 8 7 4 2
        ♡ Q 10 7 4
        ◇ —                          EAST
        ♣ K 10 5 4               ♠ A Q 3
                                 ♡ 9
                                 ◇ J 10 9 7 4 3
                                 ♣ J 8 3
```

Bidding

SOUTH	WEST	NORTH	EAST
1 ♠	Double	4 ♠	Double
Pass	Pass	Pass	

Partner leads a small heart and declarer wins with the king. He leads the jack of spades and lets it ride when partner shows out, discarding a club. Partner surely has the ace of clubs for his double. Should you return a club right away to get your heart ruff? That is what the actual East player did, but his partner returned a club in an effort to give him a club ruff. To avoid this play, East should return a diamond upon winning the first spade trick. When he gets in again, he can return a club, and West will know it was not a singleton club since it was not returned at the first opportunity. Consequently he would return a heart for two reasons: It is the only chance, and if East had a doubleton heart, he would have returned his remaining heart instead of a diamond at the third trick. Declarer's hand was

♠ J 10 9 x x ♡ A K x x x ◇ K x ♣ x,

leaving partner with

♠ — ♡ J x x ◇ A Q x x x ♣ A Q x x x.

Occasionally it is necessary to deceive partner in order to direct the defense along the right lines.

NORTH
♠ K J 9 7 4
♡ Q 6
◇ Q J 5
♣ A K 8

EAST
♠ 8 3
♡ A 7 4 2
◇ A K 10 8 7 6 3
♣ —

Bidding

EAST	SOUTH	WEST	NORTH
1 ◇	1 ♠	Pass	4 ♠
Pass	Pass	Pass	

Partner leads the nine of diamonds, covered by the jack. The natural impulse is to play the king, but if you look ahead, you will play the ace. Next you cash the ace of hearts. Partner gives you the ten, so you know two things: he has the king, and he still has a diamond left. If he wanted a diamond ruff, he would not encourage you in hearts. Partner wins the next heart trick with the king (declarer playing the jack) and goes into a long study. Partner's hand was

♠ x ♡ K 10 9 x x ◇ x x ♣ 10 9 x x x.

With one more spade, he would be tempted to return a diamond so that you could give him a ruff for a two-trick set, if you should hold the ace of spades. But a diamond return is futile with only one spade left when he "knows" declarer has the king of diamonds. Could a heart return be right? Were you trying for a heart ruff? A heart return looks futile with such good trumps in the dummy. Partner's only hope to accomplish something is to return a club. If you had won the first diamond trick with the king, it would never have occurred to partner that he should return anything but a diamond upon winning with the king of hearts.

The following hand appears in Terence Reese's *Master Play*, a very excellent book for advanced players. It is unusual in that East has a choice of false-cards available to direct the defense.

NORTH
♠ Q 6 5 3
♡ K 8 4 2
◇ A
♣ K J 10 4

WEST
♠ 7 4
♡ Q J
◇ 8 6 3 2
♣ A 9 8 5 2

EAST
♠ A K J 10 2
♡ 9
◇ J 10 9 5
♣ 7 6 3

SOUTH
♠ 9 8
♡ A 10 7 6 5 3
◇ K Q 7 4
♣ Q

Bidding

NORTH	EAST	SOUTH	WEST
1 ♣	1 ♠	2 ♡	Pass
4 ♡	Pass	Pass	Pass

West leads a small spade. East's best chance might well be to play his partner for a singleton spade and the ace of clubs or a promotable trump trick, but East guesses correctly that partner and declarer have two spades each. He wants the ace of clubs to be cashed before continuing spades. As can be seen, this is the only successful line of defense. So East wins the ten of spades and returns a club. West wins—but he returns a club, figuring his partner for six spades and a singleton club. As Mr. Reese points out, if East had a singleton club, he should win the first spade trick with the ace to discourage a spade return. Also West might well have asked himself where the setting trick was going to come from unless declarer had another spade. However, East can make it very easy for his partner by winning the first spade with the *jack*. Now declarer is "marked" with the ten, and West has a sure set by returning a spade.

CHAPTER V

Inferences From the
Opponents' Play

THE MOST dangerous inferences to draw are those from the way the opponents play or defend. On rare occasions a skillful opponent will anticipate your problem and lead you astray with an imaginative and deceptive line of play. However, you are more frequently led astray by the mistakes and illogical plays of the opponents than by their brilliancies.

When an opposing declarer continues to play trumps after you and your partner have no more, you assume that he has no losers which could be ruffed. This is a fairly safe assumption to make in any game. Can you infer that your side suit is stacked when the opening lead is a trump? Can you infer that a suit is not establishable when the opponents defend passively or make no effort to kill your entries? It depends entirely upon the skill of your opponents. Sometimes you take a wrong view because of overestimating or underestimating their skill.

In this chapter, most of the inferences are safe for you to draw against average opponents. In a few cases you should not make the recommended play unless your opponents are quite expert.

NORTH
♠ A Q 10 8
♡ 6   *Match-point duplicate: bidding*
◇ A Q 7 4 3

NORTH	EAST	SOUTH	WEST
1 ◇	Pass	1 ♡	Pass
1 ♠	Pass	2 NT	Pass
3 NT	Pass	Pass	Pass

♣ A 6 5

SOUTH
♠ 9 7
♡ A K 5
◇ J 10 9 6
♣ K 8 4 2

West leads the queen of hearts. You win the very first trick since if everything works, you have all thirteen tricks, and a duck in hearts is very unlikely to do any good. When the jack of diamonds is led, West covers. As you run three more diamond tricks, West discards two hearts and a club while East discards one spade. You take the deep spade finesse and East wins with the jack. Naturally he returns a heart. At rubber bridge this hand would not present a problem. In duplicate you don't know whether to settle for ten tricks or try for twelve. You lead another spade and West plays the six. If he has just the king left, you can take all the rest of the tricks by finessing, but if the finesse loses, you may be forced to discard a winner or two on the opponents' good hearts. If West started with K x x of spades, then East started with J x x x. Would he throw away a spade? It is very unlikely, because at the time he made his discard, he could not have known who had the king of spades unless it was in his own hand. East's spade holding was K J x x.

NORTH
♠ Q 6
♡ K Q 8 6
◇ A 7 4 3
♣ K 7 3

Match-point duplicate

SOUTH
♠ A 10 5
♡ A 7 5 3 2
◇ K 8 2
♣ A 4

The opening lead against your four-heart contract is a small club. You draw the adverse trumps in two rounds, followed by the ace and king of diamonds, the king of clubs, and a club ruff. Then you lead a third diamond, West winning with the queen, and East dropping the jack. West then leads a small spade. What do you play? If your opponents are good players, you must play small from dummy on the assumption that East has the king of spades. If West had the king of spades, he would have unblocked the queen of diamonds. If East had held the queen of diamonds but had unblocked so that West would now be on lead, you would be positive that East had the king of spades.

NORTH
♠ K J 5 4 2
♡ A 7
◇ K 10 5
♣ 8 7 4

SOUTH
♠ A Q 8 7 3
♡ 5 4
◇ A 8 4
♣ Q 10 6

Bidding

SOUTH	WEST	NORTH	EAST
1 ♠	Double	Redouble	2 ♡
Pass	3 ♡	3 ♠	Pass
Pass	Pass		

West leads the king of clubs and switches to the jack of hearts. The ace wins, and you draw trumps in two rounds, West discarding a heart. A heart is led, won by East with the queen. He returns a club, and West cashes the jack and ace. West then returns a small diamond. What do you play from dummy? It is tempting to play small, hoping that West has led from the queen-nine or jack-nine. Your correct play is the ten of diamonds if West is a good player. Your only legitimate chance to make the hand is to find West with the queen-jack of diamonds. With queen-nine or jack-nine, he should lead the honor. West's actual hand:

♠ x   ♡ K J 10 x   ◇ Q J x x   ♣ A K J x

NORTH
♠ A K 9
♡ A 5 4
◇ 10 4
♣ K Q 7 6 4

SOUTH
♠ J 10 6 3
♡ K J 9
◇ A K 8 3
♣ A 10

Bidding

SOUTH	WEST	NORTH	EAST
1 NT	Pass	6 NT	Pass
Pass	Pass		

West leads a small heart, which you win with the nine. West does not look very happy about this. You lead a spade to the dummy in order to finesse the ten of clubs. West wins and returns a spade. You had planned to take the spade finesse if you should lose a club trick, but it is time to reconsider. West already gave you one trick on opening lead. He could never look his partner in the eye if he were to give you another trick and the contract by leading from the queen of spades. He cannot possibly know that you have the ten of spades, and he surely has a safe exit in clubs. You win with the king of spades, and play a club to the ace. You cash the king and ace of hearts and run the clubs. Fortunately East is squeezed, having started with

♠ Q x x x   ♡ x x   ◇ J 9 x x x   ♣ x x.

You did not know that a squeeze would work; you merely knew that the spade finesse would *not* work, so you had to look for an alternate line of play.

NORTH
♠ 10 8 7 6 4
♡ 6 3
◇ A 10 8 5
♣ 7 5

Bidding

SOUTH	WEST	NORTH	EAST
1 ♠	Double	4 ♠	Pass
Pass	Pass		

SOUTH
♠ K J 9 5 2
♡ K 7 4
◇ K
♣ A 10 6 3

West leads the king of clubs, which you permit to hold the trick, and he shifts to a low diamond. You play the eight from dummy; East plays the jack, and you win with the king. Next you cash the ace of clubs and lead another club upon which West discards a heart. You ruff in dummy and return a spade. East plays the queen, you cover, and West wins with the ace. West then returns another diamond. A successful finesse of the ten will give you two tricks for two heart discards. Should you take the finesse? Not if West is a good player. If the diamond finesse were going to work for you, he would have exited with his last spade. The reason he led the diamond was to induce you to put in the ten because he knew that his partner's queen could be ruffed out otherwise. West's hand:

♠ A x   ♡ A J x x   ◇ x x x x x   ♣ K Q

NORTH
♠ K 10 4
♡ J 5
◇ K 7 4 3 2   *Bidding*
♣ Q 7 3

SOUTH	WEST	NORTH	EAST
1 NT	Pass	3 NT	Pass
Pass	Pass		

SOUTH
♠ 7 6
♡ K 8 6 2
◇ A Q 10
♣ A K 9 4

The opening lead is the five of spades. The ten loses to East's jack, and he returns the nine of spades. West wins with the ace and returns the three of spades, East following with the deuce. West apparently had five spades to the ace-queen. Why didn't he duck the second round to preserve an entry? It must be because he has a sure side entry, obviously the ace of hearts. Right now you are not particularly concerned about the ace of hearts, but you soon will be. You lay down the ace and queen of diamonds and East discards a heart on the second round. Now you can only count seven sure tricks, but if you can develop four club tricks, you should have West on some sort of squeeze. What is the best chance to take four club tricks? Since West has five spades and four diamonds, the odds are that he will be short in clubs. Consequently you cash the ace and lead to the queen. When West drops the ten, you successfully finesse the nine and lead the king. On the third and fourth rounds of clubs West discards his remaining spades. A diamond is led to the king followed by the fourth round of diamonds. West wins and has to give you a heart trick. No other defense would have worked for him, since his hand was

♠ A Q x x x   ♡ A Q   ◇ J 9 x x   ♣ 10 x.

If his hearts had been A x instead of A Q, he probably would have discarded a spade and a heart. But, knowing his distribution, and playing him for the ace of hearts, you would then have led a low heart before cashing the king of diamonds.

```
        NORTH
    ♠ K Q 7 6 3
    ♡ A 9
    ◇ 7 4                      Bidding
    ♣ J 8 7 3       EAST    SOUTH    WEST    NORTH
                    1 ◇     2 ♡      Pass    3 ♡
        SOUTH       Pass    4 ♡      Pass    Pass
    ♠ A 4 2         Pass
    ♡ Q J 10 8 6 2
    ◇ 10 5
    ♣ A Q
```

West leads the three of diamonds, won by East with the jack. He returns the five of spades. Surely his only purpose in leading a spade is to try for a ruff. It looks as though East has the king of hearts, and West may well have a diamond honor as an entry to give East his ruff. If East is missing a diamond honor, probably the king, he ought to have the king of clubs for his opening bid. The correct play is to win the spade return in dummy, finesse the queen of clubs, and cash the ace. A heart is then led to the ace, followed by the jack of clubs and a diamond discard. East wins this trick but is unable to put his partner on lead for the spade ruff. East's hand:

♠ x   ♡ K x x   ◇ A Q J x x   ♣ K x x x

```
        NORTH
    ♠ K 8 5
    ♡ Q 10 5                   Bidding
    ◇ K Q J 8 4    SOUTH    WEST      NORTH       EAST
    ♣ J 5          1 ♡      Double    Redouble    2 ♣
                   Pass     3 ♣       3 ♡         Pass
        SOUTH      4 ♡      Pass      Pass        Pass
    ♠ A Q 7 2
    ♡ A J 9 4 3
    ◇ 6 5 2
    ♣ 7
```

West leads the seven of diamonds, and the king wins the trick, East playing the three. How do you think the diamonds are split? West surely has the ace for his bidding. Would he underlead the ace three-long or four-long with the ace-king of clubs? An ace is seldom underled when there is a safe alternative. Also, if West had underled A x x of diamonds, wouldn't East play a high diamond to indicate a doubleton? East cannot possibly want a switch so his failure to play a higher diamond definitely indicates that he does not have a doubleton. If East has a singleton diamond, West has four, together with at least four clubs for the club raise. With so few high cards, West would not make a take-out double if he were short in spades. It is *conceivable,* but very unlikely, that West holds

$$\spadesuit \text{ J x x x } \heartsuit \text{ x } \diamondsuit \text{ A x x x } \clubsuit \text{ A Q x x.}$$

More likely, since West is apparently missing a club honor, he holds the king of hearts. With four diamonds and four clubs he cannot hold three hearts, so there is no point in refusing the heart finesse if East has a singleton diamond.

A possibility which may not have occurred to you is that West led the seven of diamonds from the doubleton ace-seven. If West is a tricky sort of player, this is the most likely holding, consistent with the bidding and play at the first trick. The best play to guard against this holding is to lead a club immediately to waste East's entry before the diamonds are unblocked. West's hand:

$$\spadesuit \text{ 10 9 x x } \heartsuit \text{ K x } \diamondsuit \text{ A x } \clubsuit \text{ A Q 10 x x}$$

Playing the ace and another trump would have worked also. When this hand was played, declarer took the heart finesse. West won, cashed the ace of diamonds and led a low club to his partner's king for a diamond ruff. While declarer might have reasoned along the lines indicated, West's play disguised his intentions as well as possible. Declarer surely would have led the ace and another heart if the opening lead had been the ace, followed by a small diamond.

NORTH
♠ A Q 9
♡ A K J
♦ 6 5
♣ K J 9 5 4

SOUTH
♠ J 7 4
♡ Q 8 7 5 4
♦ 8 3
♣ A 6 2

Bidding

NORTH	EAST	SOUTH	WEST
1 ♣	Pass	1 ♡	Pass
1 ♠	Pass	2 ♣	Pass
3 ♡	Pass	4 ♡	Pass
Pass	Pass		

West cashes the king and queen of diamonds, then shifts to a low spade. You duck, and East wins with the king. He then leads a third round of diamonds. The opponents should be able to figure out your distribution. If they are willing to give you a sluff and ruff, it is probably because it will not help you. You should take the ruff in your hand to guard against a 4–1 trump break. This is simply a case of not accepting a Greek gift.

I hope that it will not distract your attention from the point I am making to say that the winning play this time would have been to ruff in dummy, discarding a club from your hand. When you were offered a sluff and ruff, you assumed that the club finesse would work, and the trumps were breaking badly. But East knew that you were a good player and would reason that way! Since he had the ten of hearts, he knew that you could not afford to ruff in dummy. He figured that you might have A 10 x of clubs (consequently a choice of plays), and his diamond return would be certain to lead you astray. What a high-level game bridge can be when you and the opponents each respect the other's ability!

NORTH
♠ K 10 9 7 6
♡ 5
♢ 5   *Bidding*
♣ A Q J 7 4 3

SOUTH	WEST	NORTH	EAST
1 ♠	2 ♡	4 NT	6 ♡

SOUTH
♠ A Q J 5 3 2

7 ♠	Pass	Pass	Double

♡ A 7 6
♢ Q J 3
♣ 10

Pass	Pass	Pass	

The seven-spade bid was slightly exuberant, but the problem is to make the hand when West leads the king of hearts. East's double said, "Don't lead a heart." (You know that he has the ace of diamonds.) Why didn't West follow his partner's instructions and lead a minor suit? It is probably because he has the guarded kings of both minors with which he thought he could beat the grand slam by defending passively, and he was afraid that a lead from the wrong king might be disastrous. Consequently you should play West for the king of clubs. The finesse is necessary because West holds

♠ x   ♡ K Q 10 x x   ♢ K x x   ♣ K x x x.

NORTH
♠ K Q 9 7 3
♡ K 6 5
♢ Q 6   *Bidding*
♣ A 6 5

SOUTH	WEST	NORTH	EAST
1 ♡	Pass	1 ♠	Pass
2 NT	Pass	3 ♡	Pass
3 ♠	Pass	4 ♣	Pass
4 ♡	Pass	6 NT	Pass

SOUTH
♠ A 8 4

Pass	Pass		

♡ A Q 10 8 3
♢ K 7
♣ K J 2

This hand was dealt in a national board-a-match team game. West leads the ten of diamonds. Dummy and East play small, and you win with the king. With good breaks, you will now have thirteen tricks. But do you expect good breaks? Your hand is not quite as strong as it should be; the 2 no-trump re-bid was a stretch. Partner was obviously trying for seven. Would a good East player duck with the ace of diamonds under these conditions if he could see that the major suits were going to break for you? (Remember this is board-a-match scoring, and one can lose a board just as easily by 30 points as by 1,500.) Incidentally, why should he duck under any conditions? It is because he doesn't know whether you have two or three diamonds. It would give you an extra trick for him to play the ace if you were to hold K x x.

The ace and king of hearts are played, with both opponents following. A third round is led, and East plays the jack while West discards a diamond. Since the hearts have broken nicely, it must be the spades that are stacked. A low spade is led to the king, followed by a low spade back. When East plays small, you put in the eight spot and take all thirteen tricks! East had

♠ J 10 x x   ♡ J x x   ◇ A J x   ♣ x x x.

If East had split his spade honors, you would have had an easy end-play by cashing all your winners outside of spades and tossing East in with the ace of diamonds. East made the right play not to split his spade honors since you might have lacked the courage to play the eight.

Defense

NORTH
♠ K 8 5
♡ A 7 6 4 3
◊ J 10 9 5
♣ K

EAST
♠ A J 4
♡ K J 8
◊ 8 7 4 2
♣ 6 4 3

North-South 60 part-score: bidding

SOUTH	WEST	NORTH	EAST
3 ♣	Pass	Pass	Pass

Partner leads the king of diamonds, won by declarer's ace. A low club is led to the king followed by a low heart back, which you win with the king. What can you tell about declarer's hand? If he has a seven-card club suit headed by the ace, it will not be possible to set him, so you must assume that not to be the case. What was declarer's original holding in diamonds? The one holding you can be sure that he did not have is A x. With a doubleton diamond he would lead back a diamond to establish a discard for a heart loser rather than concede a heart trick. If declarer had A x x of diamonds he would not continue diamonds for fear of a ruff. So you should lead a diamond yourself. Partner wins and returns a low spade. You take, in all, two spade tricks, one heart trick, one diamond trick, and a ruff. Declarer's hand:

♠ x x   ♡ x x   ◊ A x x   ♣ A Q 10 9 x x

NORTH
♠ A 7 5
♡ A K Q 4 3
◇ 6
♣ A 7 5 3

WEST
♠ K Q 9 8
♡ J 9 8 6
◇ K 8
♣ Q 6 2

Bidding

NORTH	EAST	SOUTH	WEST
1 ♡	Pass	2 ◇	Pass
3 ♣	Pass	3 ◇	Pass
3 NT	Pass	5 ◇	Pass
Pass	Pass		

You lead the king of spades, won by dummy's ace. Partner drops the jack. Declarer then leads a diamond to his queen, and you win with the king. As it happens, you would have preferred to have partner show his distribution at the first trick rather than let you know that you can put him in with the ten of spades, but partner made the signal which would normally be most valuable to you. It is very unlikely that declarer started with three small spades. If he did, he would have tried to discard one of them on the hearts before taking the trump finesse. So you shift to a club. Declarer's hand:

♠ x x   ♡ x x   ◇ A Q J x x x   ♣ x x

Declarer cannot get back to his hand and is forced to play for a 3–3 heart break, which does not develop. Obviously, cashing a spade when you got in with the king of diamonds would have given declarer the contract by permitting him a ruffing entry to his hand to draw trumps.

NORTH
♠ K 6 5
♡ A 6
◇ 10 8 7 6
♣ 10 7 5 4

EAST
♠ J 10 7 4 2
♡ 7
◇ Q J 3
♣ Q 8 6 2

Bidding

SOUTH	WEST	NORTH	EAST
1 ♡	Pass	1 NT	Pass
4 ♡	Pass	Pass	Pass

Partner leads the nine of spades. Declarer wins with the ace. He cashes the king of hearts and queen of spades. When he leads a trump to the ace, partner plays the nine and you discard a spade. The king of spades is led, declarer discarding a small diamond. He then leads a club to his king, losing to partner's ace. Partner returns the jack of clubs.

What can you tell about the distribution at this point? If declarer had an eight-card trump suit, he is cold for his contract with an overtrick, and it would make no difference what you play. Consequently you must assume that he has just seven hearts. Why did partner fail to return a trump? It must be because he has the one trump holding that can be promoted by an over-ruff threat, in other words, the jack. Declarer must be placed with ace-queen alone of spades and seven hearts to the king-queen-ten. What is his distribution in the minors? If it were 3–1, he would have discarded his singleton, ruffed back to his own hand, and drawn trumps for a cold ten tricks. So declarer must have had two cards in each minor. He has discarded one diamond and will follow to this trick with his last club. Your correct play is to overtake partner's jack of clubs and lead your remaining spade. If declarer discards his remaining diamond on this trick instead of ruffing, partner will discard his last club. You can then promote partner's jack of trumps with a club lead. Declarer's hand:

♠ A Q   ♡ K Q 10 x x x x   ◇ K x   ♣ K x

NORTH
♠ Q 6
♡ K 8 5
◇ A K 8 4
♣ 8 6 5 2

EAST
♠ K 10 7 3
♡ Q J 7
◇ Q 10 6
♣ K J 4

Bidding

NORTH	EAST	SOUTH	WEST
1 NT*	Pass	2 ♣	Pass
2 ◇	Pass	3 ♡	Pass
4 ♡	Pass	Pass	Pass

* weak

Partner leads the two of spades, covered by the queen, king and ace. Declarer immediately leads a diamond and puts in the eight. What is he trying to do? He must have three diamonds (it would be pointless to duck with any other number) and he hopes to set up the thirteenth diamond for a discard. What does he want to discard? It must be a club since he can ruff his third spade. So you should return a club immediately. Declarer has the ace, but he is in trouble anyway. His hand is

♠ A x x   ♡ A x x x x   ◇ x x x   ♣ A x.

He cannot use the thirteenth diamond without drawing the trumps, and if he draws the trumps, he loses his spade ruff. His best chance is to play the two high trumps and run the diamonds. On the thirteenth diamond, you must refuse to ruff, but when a low spade is led from dummy, you hop in with the ten to pull another round of trumps. A spade return, or anything other than a club, at the third trick would enable declarer to ruff his spade loser, pull two rounds of trumps and take his club discard while you watched helplessly.

```
                                NORTH
                                ♠ K 6
                                ♡ K 8 5
            WEST                ◇ 9 6 3
            ♠ 7 5               ♣ K J 10 9 4
            ♡ A J 9
            ◇ K 10 7 4 2
            ♣ 8 6 3
```

Bidding

SOUTH	WEST	NORTH	EAST
1 NT	Pass	3 NT	Pass
Pass	Pass		

Your opening lead is the four of diamonds. Partner plays the queen and declarer wins with the ace. At trick two declarer leads a small heart to dummy's king. Why is declarer attacking hearts instead of clubs? It is because his clubs are already established, and he is trying to steal a trick. Your proper play is to take the ace and lay down the king of diamonds. The jack drops, and you can run the suit. Actually you could be pretty sure the jack would drop. With an original diamond holding of A J x, declarer would have entered the dummy with a spade or club and led a low heart toward his hand in an effort to get *East* to duck. If you had the ace, he would be safe.

```
                    NORTH
              ♠ 9 8 5
              ♡ K 6 5
              ◊ K J 6 5                    EAST
              ♣ A 6 3                 ♠ Q J 6 3
                                      ♡ A J 3
                                      ◊ 8 5 4
                                      ♣ 8 4 2
```

Bidding

WEST	NORTH	EAST	SOUTH
Pass	Pass	Pass	1 ♡
2 ◊	Double	Pass	2 NT
Pass	3 NT	Pass	Pass
Pass			

Partner leads the deuce of spades and South captures your jack with the king. He leads a low diamond to the king and returns a low heart from dummy. What is going on? Isn't this a strange line of play? Declarer is attacking partner's diamond suit with a singleton diamond (as shown by both partner's overcall and declarer's take-out of the double). The only holding which would make this line of play logical is a six-card club suit. Can declarer have six clubs? If his bidding is uninhibited but his play is sound, you must take the ace of hearts. Declarer's hand:

     ♠ K 10   ♡ Q 10 x x   ◊ x   ♣ K Q J x x x

This hand was not just created out of my imagination. I actually bid and played declarer's hand as indicated in a Mixed Pair event at the 1961 Spring Nationals and the East player, who probably had never been faced with this sort of problem, played low.

NORTH
- ♠ Q 4
- ♡ 6 4
- ◇ 8 7 5
- ♣ K Q J 10 4 3

WEST
- ♠ K 8 6 5 2
- ♡ A 8 3
- ◇ K 2
- ♣ 9 8 7

Bidding

SOUTH	WEST	NORTH	EAST
1 ♡	Pass	2 ♣	Pass
2 ◇	Pass	3 ♣	Pass
3 NT	Pass	Pass	Pass

Your opening lead is the five of spades. Dummy wins with the queen, and partner plays the nine. A heart is led to declarer's ten, and you take the ace. What can you figure out about this hand? Let's start with spades. Partner cannot have the ace of spades, or he would have won the opening lead. If he had J 10 9 of spades, he would have played the jack. With the ten-nine of spades, if he were to signal at all, he would play the ten (which would deny the jack). Therefore partner must have the jack-nine-small of spades, leaving declarer with A 10 x. Why would declarer risk playing the queen of spades when he would have a sure double stopper by playing low? He must have needed to be in the dummy very badly, and this was his only chance to get there. The ten of hearts must have been a finesse. With

♠ A 10 x　♡ K Q 10 x x　◇ A Q x x　♣ x

would declarer have bid three no-trump over three clubs? With no fit for clubs, no running suit, and only a single spade stopper, he would have to be a wild man to bid it. Even with the additional jack of diamonds, it would be an optimistic bid. More likely declarer's singleton club is the ace. With all these factors in mind, you are going to have to defend very carefully to avoid being end-played. The best solution is to lead the king of spades. Declarer's hand:

♠ A 10 x   ♡ K Q 10 x x   ◇ A Q x x   ♣ A

A careless return of a low spade would be fatal. Declarer would surely cash the ace of clubs and his heart tricks, then put you on lead with a spade. As it happens, declarer can make the hand even with the king of spades return, but only by adopting an abnormal line of play.

NORTH
♠ A J 9 7 6 4
♡ J 6
◇ A J 5
♣ 5 3

EAST
♠ K 10
♡ Q 4 3
◇ Q 9 8 4
♣ K 8 7 2

Bidding

SOUTH	WEST	NORTH	EAST
1 NT*	Pass	3 ♠	Pass
3 NT	Pass	Pass	Pass

* weak

Partner leads a low heart, declarer holding off with the ace until the third round, and discarding a diamond from dummy. From the heart spots you can tell partner had a five-card suit. Declarer then plays a low spade and finesses the jack. You should play the ten as though you had no problem.* Declarer's play of the spade suit marks him with Q x x. If he had two or three

---

* Actually it is not necessary to be a fast thinker when declarer leads the first spade to the jack. You should have done all your thinking and planning when you won the queen of hearts at trick one! The expert makes a practice of planning his defense at a time when no particular inference can be drawn from his pause. He is then prepared to play smoothly and surely at the crucial moment.

small, he would finesse the nine since the contract would be unmakeable if partner holds both the king and queen—declarer must keep your partner off lead at all costs. With Q x, declarer would lead the queen. For one thing, he would not want to block the suit. If the queen were covered, he would finesse the nine next time. This would be the best play to develop the suit while keeping your partner off lead.

When the jack of spades holds the trick, dropping your ten, declarer is certain to adopt the wrong line of play. He returns to his hand with the ace of clubs, spurning any possible finesse, to lead the queen of spades through partner's "marked" king. It is now easy to read declarer's hand. If he had had the king of diamonds, he surely would have come back to it for the spade finesse, rather than release the ace of clubs. Therefore, when you win the king of spades, you cash the king of clubs and exit with a diamond. Declarer's hand:

♠ Q x x   ♡ A x x   ◊ 10 x x   ♣ A Q 10 x